D1505037

Architecture from the Outside

Writing **Architecture** *Series*

A project of the Anyone Corporation

The MIT Press Cambridge, Massachusetts London, England

Architecture from the Outside

Essays on Virtual and Real Space

Elizabeth Grosz  Peter Eisenman

foreword by

© 2001 Massachusetts Institute of Technology

All rights reserved. No part of this book may be reproduced in any form by any electronic or mechanical means (including photocopying, recording, or information storage and retrieval) without permission in writing from the publisher.

This book was set in Janson Text and Franklin Gothic by Graphic Composition, Inc., Athens, Georgia, and was printed and bound in the United States of America.

Library of Congress Cataloging-in-Publication Data

Grosz, E. A. (Elizabeth A.)
  Architecture from the outside : essays on virtual and real space / Elizabeth Grosz.
  p. cm. — (Writing architecture)
  Includes bibliographical references and index.
  ISBN 0-262-57149-8 (pbk. : alk. paper)
  1. Architecture—Philosophy. 2. Space (Architecture)—Philosophy. I. Title. II. Series.
NA2500 .G76 2001
  720′.1—dc21   2001018300

I am an outsider to the field of architecture. My access to this field was facilitated in a most indirect and unexpected way, for research and writing in this area is something I never expected or directed myself toward with any confidence or self-consciousness. It was only in retrospect, after a period of some eight or nine years, that it became clear to me that architecture and its associated questions of space, spatiality, and inhabitation held too much fascination not to

Acknowledgments

be addressed in more depth. This collection exists largely due to the support and encouragement of Cynthia Davidson, to her extended invitations to participate in the Any annual conferences, which she so creatively convened and conceptually formulated over a ten-year period, and to her encouragement in gathering my work as a volume in the Writing Architecture series for the MIT Press. She helped me see that a productive interchange between philosophy and architecture can work for the mutual enrichment, and opening out, of both historically distinct disciplines, and that philosophy needs to think more carefully about architecture as much as architecture is capable of augmentation by philosophy. I would also like to single out John Rajchman for his long-term vision of the relations between postmodern theory and contemporary architectural reflection, which has inspired and energized me to think about this book and the various papers that comprise it. Our ongoing conversations have always been illuminating, edifying, challenging, and rewarding. I would like to thank Victor Burgin and Beatriz Colomina for taking the risk over a decade ago of asking a complete architectural novice to turn her attentions to the question of space, initiating a process which, unforeseeably and for better or worse, led to the piecemeal production of this book. My thanks also to Peter Eisenman, Bernard Tschumi, and Anthony Vidler for their benevolence and welcoming tolerance of the outsider that philosophers tend to be, especially to architectural practice and writing.

The support of institutions during the writing of papers and books is crucial and also deserves acknowledgment. I would like to thank the Critical Theory and Cultural Studies Program at Monash University, Melbourne, Australia, where I worked from 1992 until 1998, for the time and inspiration they provided me to write the majority of the papers gathered here. I would like to acknowledge the support and encouragement provided me for this truly hybrid and interdisciplinary project by the two interdisciplinary places I have worked since leaving Monash—the Critical Theory Program at the University of California, Irvine, and the Comparative Literature Department at the State University of New York at Buffalo. I would especially like to thank the various students of architecture and the visual arts to whom I presented many of these papers before they were ready for publication. One's texts are only ever as good, if one is lucky, as one's audience, and I have been privileged to be involved with a number of exciting and challenging audiences and interlocutors to whom I owe thanks for helping me to sharpen these papers in the process of rewriting them for this book. All the papers have been modified, changed, and in some cases updated, although they are presented here in the order in which they were written, with no attempt to remove disagreements and points of uneasiness between papers and no attempt to remove the transformation within my arguments as they developed over many years.

Acknowledgments

Without a large network of friends—colleagues and critics—one risks the kind of confrontation with limits and frustrations that may drive a would-be author to despair and even madness at the vastness, impossibility, and presumptuousness of the process of writing, let alone writing in order to invite and create the new. Here Gai Stern, Philipa Rothfield, Jacqueline Reid, and Judith Allen deserve my continuing gratitude for their humor, friendship, and loyalty. Pheng Cheah, as always, has provided intelligence and insight into my work. Nicole Fermon not only has been an ongoing source of insight and inspiration but has also provided the encouragement and strength I needed to understand that struggle—political and conceptual, with oneself and with others—is the condition of everything worthwhile, and that courage is necessary to think, to write, and especially to think and write as an outsider—a position that makes one especially vulnerable to criticism, but also fresh and new to the inside.

Finally, I would like to dedicate this book to my parents, Imre and Eva Gross.

In an important essay published in 1979, the architectural historian Manfredo Tafuri distinguished between two types of history. The first acknowledged the epistemological rupture that was inherent in industrial civiliza- tion, while the other, utopian theory, he saw as hidden in the functionalism of Sigfried Giedion and the anticlassicism of Bruno Zevi. These latter histories, which Tafuri labeled as operative or normative criticism, became the continuing apologia for the utopian vision of the modern movement. Whatever the formal nature of its urban vision, from megastructures to townscape, utopia was the underlying theory of synthesis. Tafuri wrote, "To untie the Gordian knot that in contemporary architecture binds design and utopia must mean to recover techniques of design capable of spotting the crisis from within." For Tafuri, this meant to dissolve the languages of architecture that were always imprisoned in a dialectical synthesis. This dissolution lay in a no-man's land, a no place, an atopia, the boundaries of which were forever shifting.

Some twenty years later, and after the supposed demise of the place of utopia in contemporary discourse, signaled by critics as disparate as Tafuri and Colin Rowe, comes an author, neither an architect nor a historian, who is willing to take up the theme of utopia once again. This time her purpose is not to further occlude the usefulness of the term, but rather to offer it a different place in which to survive. Her argument is not so much based on history and historicized utopias as on an alternative concept, that of the time of space and ultimately that of duration, the time of an object.

Elizabeth Grosz does not simply recite the well-worn pages of Gilles Deleuze, Jacques Derrida, or Henri Bergson on the subject of duration. Rather her attempt is to open up a central thematic of modernist architecture—utopia—to a new consideration. Grosz, like Tafuri, suggests that utopia is the good place that is no place. She says that utopia might be the way for architecture to find its own place in the political by reconceptualizing itself as that movement of time which is duration: a concept of time as a perpetual becoming. For her this becoming is that of the becoming embodied. Instead of freezing time into an arrangement of space as an ideal of the present, Grosz suggests that time is the division of duration, is the very condition of simultaneity.

Her essay "Embodied Utopias: The Time of Architecture," one of nine in this book, is central to her approach. She is a philosopher writing about issues in which architecture appears as a central problematic, one adumbrated but not exhausted by such poststructuralist writers as Derrida, Deleuze, and Luce Irigaray. When Grosz wanders closest to architecture and away from the security of philosophy is when she becomes most interesting and at the same time most problematic. "Embodied Utopias" is enlightening in this respect, particularly with the precision and clarity of the writing; but it is clearly coming from philosophy, not architecture, because the reader has to fill in his or her own specific references to current architectural thought on the subject.

Her two contributions to the discussion of utopia center on the embodiment of time and in particular that of gender. It is here that she makes her most contemporary arguments. For Grosz, utopia is a system of reason that is incapable of realizing its own systematicity. Therefore the term *embodied utopia* becomes paradoxical. It is nondialectical in a spatial sense, and nonlinear in a temporal sense. Utopia elides the question of time and futurity. Grosz says that until the dimension of time or duration has an impact on the ways in which architecture is theorized and practiced, the utopic, with its dual impossibility and necessity, will remain outside architecture's reach.

In the division of duration into past and present, the past is seen as a virtuality of the present, while the future is that which overwrites or restructures the virtual that is the past. Duration is that flow which connects the future to the past. In this sense, she is saying that the utopian is not a projection of the future; rather, it is the projection of a past or present as if it were a virtual future. For Grosz, the error in utopian thought and imagery is that it mistakes a possibility for a virtuality, and thus fails to conceive of utopia as a temporality. This can be seen, she writes, in the cities of Canberra and Brasília, which are each functional but unlivable.

Grosz's major breakthrough comes with the idea of embodiment. Here she differs from both Tafuri's and Rowe's critiques of utopia. For Grosz, embodiment means a multiplicity of bodies, contrary to the hierarchical teleology of most utopian ideals. Ideals for her are a process, a measure of dissatisfaction with the past and the present. Embodiment becomes a gendered idea, but only as an attitude of endless questioning. It is within this questioning, she believes, that architecture can come to terms with its own phallocentrism. For Grosz the embodiment of the virtual, the condition of a possible utopia, means the inclusion of the other. In this context, the other is not only the feminine but all virtualities not actualized in any present or presence. Architecture as a metaphysics of presence and the present is always already an embodiment and at the same time, in order to be a critique of its own phallocentrism, must be a disavowal of this embodiment. It is the simultaneous acceptance of architecture's being as a functioning entity and the necessary critique of this instrumentalism that brings Grosz to a parallel concept of utopia, that of the in-between. This is an idea of interval that is both virtual—that is, it is neither spatial nor temporal—and at the same time singular, and thus autonomous to architecture.

It is with the concept of autonomy that Grosz finally distinguishes architecture from philosophy. The in-between becomes the vehicle that is not a literal spatial fact but rather a cognitive and critical model. The in-between is different in architecture, for example, than in either painting or music. In painting, the junction between two color fields can create a halation—an afterimage at the contiguous edges of the fields that produces a retinal stimulation. The same can be said of music, where the reverberation of sound produces another form of aftereffect—the echo. The in-between in architectural space is not a literal perceptual or audible sensation, but an affective somatic response that is felt by the body in space. This feeling is not one arising from fact, but rather from the virtual possibility of architectural space. It is the fraying of the possible edges of any identity's limits. It is the undoing of the bounding conditions of presence. Such a possibility does not exist in philosophic or linguistic space but only in architecture. It is this singularity that distinguishes the philosophic idea of utopia from the architectural one. Only in architecture can the idea of an embodied and temporal virtuality be both thought and experienced. It is this idea that Grosz opens here for us, exposing past utopias to their linguistic and philosophic fallacies and limitations, and to the fact that they were not states but rather processes exploring the dim outlines of futurity.

Peter Eisenman

The outside is a peculiar place, both paradoxical and perverse. It is paradoxical insofar as it can only ever make sense, have a place, in reference to what it is not and can never be—an inside, a within, an interior. And it is perverse, for while it is placed always relative to an inside, it observes no faith to the consistency of this inside. It is perverse in its breadth, in its refusal to be contained or constrained by the self-consistency of the inside. The outside is the place one can never occupy fully or completely, for it is always other, different, at a distance from where one is. One cannot be outside everything, always outside: to be outside something is always to be inside something else. To be outside (something) is to afford oneself the possibility of a perspective, to look upon this inside, which is made difficult, if not impossible, from the inside. This is the rare and unexpected joy of outsideness: to see what cannot be seen from the inside, to be removed from the immediacy of immersion that affords no distance. However, this always occurs at a cost: to see what cannot be seen is to be unable to experience this inside in its own terms. Something is lost—the immediate intimacy of an inside position; and something is gained—the ability to critically evaluate that position and to possibly compare it with others.

This book is, in part, an exploration of the ways in which two disciplines and enterprises that are fundamentally outside of each other—architecture and philosophy—require a third space in which to interact without hierarchy, a space or position outside both, a space that doesn't yet exist. To explore architecture philosophically would entail submitting architectural design, construction, and theory to the requirements and exigencies of philosophical discourse, the rigor of philosophical argument, and the abstraction of philosophical speculation. And to examine philosophy architecturally would require using philosophical concepts and propositions, wrenched from their own theoretical context and transformed, perhaps mutilated, for architectural purposes. In either case, one discipline would submit the other to its internal needs and constraints, reducing it to its subordinated other. It is only by submitting *both* to a third term, to a position or place outside of both, that they can be explored *beside* each other, as equivalent and interconnected discourses and practices. That third space, which I call the outside, has rarely been theorized, but it has been utilized increasingly in the last few decades in the ever-growing productive interchange between postmodern philosophy and postwar architectural discourse and practice.

Exploring architecture "from the outside" is not the literal analysis of the facades or the exterior of buildings! Instead, the outside here reflects both the position of the author—an interested outsider, not trained in architecture, who is concerned about the inside from the point of view of the outside, who doesn't work within the discipline but outside it—and the position of the various discourses or frameworks adopted here, which are all in some sense outside the mainstreams of both architecture and philosophy, at the point where each reaches its current extremes. Outside each of the disciplines in their most privileged and accepted forms, outside the doxa and received conceptions, where they become experiment and innovation more than good sense with guaranteed outcomes, we will find the most perilous, experimental, and risky of texts and practices.

There is a third sense in which the outside must be invoked here. The position of the outsider—the alien or inassimilable being, the stranger—is also of direct relevance to my concerns here. While concepts of the social, the cultural, the collective, and the communal have always oriented architectural interests, it is the outside condition of the community—the alien or the stranger—that serves to cohere and solidify a community as an inside. The place of the destitute, the homeless, the sick and the dying, the place of social and cultural outsiders—including women and minorities of all kinds—must also be the concern of the architectural and the urban just as it has been of philosophy and politics.

I don't want to suggest that the position of the outsider is always or only negative, or necessarily critical, or bound up in envy, a yearning for an inside position. The outside is capable of great positivity and innovation. The outside of one field is the inside of another. Outside of architecture may be technologies, bodies, fantasies, politics, economics, and other factors that it plays on but doesn't direct or control. Outside architecture is always inside bodies, sexualities, history, culture, nature—all those others it seeks to exclude but which are the constitutive edges, the boundaries, of its operations. By invoking these limits, the limits beyond which architecture cannot function and which it can never directly control, I do not want to suggest that architecture is itself outside politics, sexuality, desire, economics: but only that these constitute its perennial sites of negotiation. However much the practitioners of architecture may seek to limit their responsibilities to these broader social and political issues, they are nevertheless deeply implicated in them and must address them in more nuanced and complex ways.

This book is a collection of ten essays written over a seven-year period, between 1994 and 2000. As such, it sits not only on the cusp of the new millennium, a transition, hopefully, from one epoch to another, but also on the cusp of new theories, concepts, and modes of representation that partake of the prevailing norms of twentieth-century thought, while openly welcoming the input of a twenty-first century whose impact has yet to emerge. The book moves through a number of philosophical and theoretical discourses that have been pertinent to architectural writings over the last decade or more: psychoanalytic theories of the split subject which reveal the fissuring of intentions, aims, and goals of subjects or agents; Derridean deconstructions of binary structures, most particularly those between form and content, origin and destination, representation and the real; Deleuzian nomadism, with its emphasis on movement, practice, and action; and Irigarayan speculations about the place of sexual difference in the past and future of architectural self-understandings.

Thematically, the book uses various philosophical frameworks, primarily those provided by Bergson, Deleuze, and Irigaray, and to a lesser extent Derrida, Simondon, Massumi, and Rajchman, to raise abstract but nonetheless nonformalistic questions about space, inhabitation, making, and building. Each chapter addresses, in quite disparate ways, the questions: How is space conventionally and architecturally understood? What are the unspoken conditions underlying such conceptions? And is it possible to see space in quite other terms, terms that render more explicit those unspoken conditions, so that it can be represented and inhabited in different ways? In other words, all of the essays collected here propose experiments, conceptual or philosophical experiments (rather than the more concrete experiments architects usually undertake), to render space and building more mobile, dynamic, and active, more as force, than they have previously been understood.

The book asks the question: How can we understand space differently, in order to organize, inhabit, and structure our living arrangements differently? It proposes two directions in searching for an answer: first, in the direction of time, duration, or temporal flow, which is usually conceptualized as the other, the outside, or the counterpart of space. My central argument throughout is that architecture, geography, and urban planning have tended to neglect or ignore temporality or to reduce it to the measurable and the calculable, that is, to space. It is central to the future of architecture that the question of time, change, and emergence become more integral to the processes of design and construction. And second, the book proposes a search in the direction of sexuality and sexual specificity. Space and building have always been conceived as sexually neutral, indifferent to sexual specificity, directed to the human—the collectively and individually human subject—which may have been conceptualized in terms of geographical, racial, or historical specificity but never in terms of sexual specificity. What does the fact that there are always and irreducibly (at least) two sexes have to do with how we understand and live space? And how does the apparent neutrality or humanness of previous conceptions of space and architecture sit with an acknowledgment of this irreducible specificity? This is to pose the question, in Irigaray's terminology, of the phallocentrism of architecture and its openness to sexual difference. These two currents of temporality and sexual specificity flow and cross each other through all the essays gathered in this collection.

The book has been divided into three sections, which are broadly in the order of the chronology of their writing. Part 1, "Embodied Spaces," is made up of three chapters. The first is a recent interview that highlights the place of "the outside" in all my work. The second, "Lived Spatiality (The Spaces of Corporeal Desire)," the earliest written, is a wildly speculative piece on the lived body and its experiences of space, the link between the imaginary anatomy and the acquisition of representations of space, as articulated by the writings of Jacques Lacan and Roger Caillois. The third chapter, "Futures, Cities, Architecture," is a brief discussion, more a sketch, of the relation between bodies and cities and their potential for being otherwise. Among them, these three essays provide a broad framework and the basic questions that all the other essays engage, elaborate, and transform.

Part 2, "Transitional Spaces," is also composed of three chapters. Chapter 4, "Architecture from the Outside," is an introductory analysis of the relevance of Deleuze's work, and especially of his conception of "the outside" for thinking about space and architecture. This notion of the outside is the core theme of the book as a whole. Chapter 5, "Cyberspace, Virtuality, and the Real: Some Architectural Reflections," explores two notions of the virtual, one developed in contemporary cybernetics and the other in Deleuze's work, and examines how one is not reducible to the other. The virtual spaces of computer programming are not spaces of the virtual, in Deleuze's sense, but the phantasmatic projections of real space. "In Between: The Natural in Architecture and Culture," chapter 6, is an attempt to reformulate and dynamize the conception of nature that has remained elided or has been considered as mere resource in architectural discourse and practice.

Part 3, "Future Spaces," is more adventurous and exploratory. Instead of outlining and providing critiques of existing models and discourses, it attempts a more thorough immersion in the profound and complex writings of Bergson and Deleuze on the relations between space and time. Chapter 7, "The Future of Space," focuses on Bergson's understanding of the virtual as that element of the past which contains the potential to generate a future different from the present and considers how architectural conceptions of space may be unhinged or complexified using a Bergsonian model of duration on space and spatial objects, reversing the usual spatialization of time with a temporalization of space. Chapter 8, "Embodied Utopias," explores the impossibility of utopian architectural ideals and how they elide the notion of duration, while chapter 9, "Architectures of Excess," examines the work of Bataille and Irigaray to understand the role of architectural excess. The final chapter, "The Thing," returns to Bergson and Deleuze and the challenges they pose to an architecture that remains resolutely related to objects and primarily to solids.

Taken as a whole, the book explores the productive intervention and immersion of bodies, and of temporality, in space and in building—the possibilities, capable of being explored through time, that bodies have of living differently in the built and the natural world. Its goal is to spark discussion, to tempt readers to think differently about space and inhabitation in order to foster other experiments in design and in thought.

May 24, 2000
New York City

Part One *Embodied Spaces*

conducted by Kim Armitage and Paul Dash

*What led you from a critical interest
in space to an interest in architecture
as a discipline?*

My interest in architecture began
a long time ago, as an undergrad-
uate or even earlier. Before I
started to write about philosophy,
I spent some years working on architectural theory and thinking
about space. Quite surprisingly
and fortuitously I received a num-
ber of invitations from schools of architecture, which en-
abled me to think a little more concretely and specifically
about space and the built environment. Later, I was invited
to a couple of architecture conferences and my "career,"
such as it is in architectural discourse, led on from there.
My interest existed all along. I simply didn't have an ap-
propriate intellectual venue or a forum to think about architecture much before that.

*What kinds of problems do you see in architecture as a discipline
given that it's one of the master discourses for speaking about
space? Do you think that it's complicit in some way with all of
those hierarchical constructions that you have written about?*

Inevitably, because every discipline is. That isn't necessarily the problem with architecture. If I were an insider in
the discipline of architecture, trained and working with
other architects, I might be able to describe to you more
clearly its critical problems. However, I am in the wonderful and unusual position of being an outsider. My dealings with the discipline have been relatively peripheral

and, for me, the beauty of those dealings as an outsider is that I've been able to do it on my terms. The problems of the discipline need to be assessed by those within it and those closer to its periphery than I am. Yet if I'd been trained as an architect, I wouldn't be able to say what I'm saying, and certainly not in the way that I have articulated it. Being outside of a discipline, though interested in its internal operations, gives one a position of relative independence and autonomy. My relations with the discipline of architecture are thus much less fraught and complicated than my relations with the discipline in which I was trained, philosophy.

So you're speaking from the outside.

I am speaking quite explicitly from the outside. To be fair to the discipline of architecture, though, it is the one discipline beyond philosophy and the humanities that is actually interested in, and in some ways committed to, what the humanities have to say. It is one of the few places that invites outside "incurşion."

So you do see architecture as outside of the humanities?

As an academic discipline, architecture *is* outside of the humanities—so in that sense there's no question that it is not one of the humanities. Not institutionally at least, even if there is something of a family resemblance. Architecture students aren't oriented to thinking, reading, and writing in quite the same way as are students within the humanities. What's interesting about architecture is that it has always been unsure as to where to position itself and its own identity as a discipline: it is itself internally divided about whether it is a science, a technological discipline, or a mode of art or aesthetic production. This uncertainty regarding its own identity has led it to be quite open to philosophical and critical theory in a way that is unimaginable for other disciplines, like engineering or medicine, for example. What I can say positively as an outsider (and I'm sure there are other things one could say) is that architecture is a discipline seeking self-definition, and for that self-definition it looks outside of itself, to see what others say about it. This, I would argue, is a very good and healthy thing.

In your writings on architecture, you imply that it has a lot to learn from philosophy: what could philosophy learn from architecture?

Surprisingly, a lot. Historically, the arrogance of philosophy has been that it has always thought of itself as the master, dominant discipline (the "queen of knowledges"), and has seen its mandate as being to look over, reflect upon, and criticize the methods of all the other disciplines. What architecture offers is something completely different; it is not a system that reflects and judges (although it does this too) but exists as a set of practices, techniques, and skills. It is much more practically mired, in rather obvious ways, than the abstraction of philosophical thinking. If philosophy could look at itself more as a process of making (as architecture explicitly thinks of itself), then it might be better off. Philosophy takes itself to be a kind of pure reflection of thought, but in fact it's an active labor of words—writing, arguing, criticizing. These are not just mental or conceptual skills but techniques of production. What is produced here is not a building or dwelling but a different mode of habitation, a text, a position, an argument or a claim. Where architects use building, bricks, mortar, stone, glass, etc., philosophers use arguments, propositions, discourses. The more humble and less imperialistic view, in fact, is the kind of pragmatism developed in architecture. We're making something, something which has material and historical limits, something that is inherently the product of collaboration and compromise, a practical experiment in living, regardless of whether we are philosophers or architects. If philosophy could think of itself more humbly as a mode of producing rather than as a mode of knowing or intellectually grasping or mastering concepts—which it can't do adequately at the moment—it would come closer to the practical nature of architectural practices, moving closer to everyday life and its concerns, which would be good for philosophy.

But it's a hard thing to do. I'm not exactly sure how it would play itself out, and what such a philosophy would look like (it does not yet exist). Architectural models have always provoked philosophy. There are some interesting and sometimes even profound metaphors within architecture that philosophy might be fascinated with (for example, notions of "dwelling" or "habitation" that so captivated Heidegger; the idea of "foundation" that fascinated Descartes and Kant; or "becoming" and "itinerancy" that beguiled Deleuze) but which philosophy really hasn't been able to come to grips with. The notion of philosophy as a making, building, production, or construction, a practical construction, is a really interesting idea, one worth developing in the future.

In your essay "Architecture from the Outside," you seem to be offering Deleuze's concepts to the field of architecture in order to "make architecture tremble." You also write that his work may force architecture to open to its outside—to sort of nudge it toward thinking—but it remained unclear to you—again because you're not in the field—precisely how that would work. Have you thought back on that and how it would work?

There are a lot of different ways in which I think Deleuze's work could take off in architecture. Whether this will happen or not, however, I cannot predict. Take the idea, for example, of building as a fixed entity or a given, stable object (which is the standard notion of building today). A Deleuzian framework may help us transform these rather static ways of understanding construction. A building is made up of other spaces within it that move and change, even if its own walls remain fixed. The idea of the mobility of building and within building is one possible idea of Deleuzian thought that might be of tremendous value in architecture. Building is not only a movement of sedimentation and stabilization but also a way of opening space and living. If you want anything more concrete than that, this is something that architects should be asked to consider.

The issues of movement are dealt with in the plan, but they are also contained: they're laid out rather than opened up.

Yes. Deleuze's idea may be useful not simply for rethinking the static or fixed plan, but also for addressing questions about what happens to a structure once it already exists. After it is built, structure is still not a fixed entity. It moves and changes, depending on how it is used, what is done with and to it, and how open it is to even further change. What sorts of metamorphoses does structure undergo when it's already there? What sorts of becomings can it engender? These kinds of issues cannot simply be accommodated or dealt with by the plan or blueprints.

Such a definition makes it difficult to think how structure might be incorporated into building.

I think it might suggest the architect relating much more to not only the current state of the design or stylistics of the building but also to its potential and future uses. How this is done, I'm not exactly sure. But the question of queer space, for example, may provide something of an illustration. There has been a lot of work invested in thinking about, planning, and developing, or even occasionally building, queer spaces. These are often community or social centers, safe spaces, and spaces of recreation, commerce, and play. Current thinking about these areas may provide an opportunity for investigating building and occupation in quite different ways. When you have a community that is open to its difference and innovation, there seems to be more scope for innovative thinking. I'm sure there are exceptions, but typically with such projects the plans involve converting existing spaces, quite commonly warehouse space, into new forms for new functions. There is then already a certain hybridity in these designs, with the renovation of existing spaces into those which function quite differently. The idea of the conversion of residual spaces implies the idea of compromise, and the idea of making do with what must be accepted while changing what remains no longer useful. There are a number of gay architects and architectural theoreticians currently working on these ideas, so I'm really not the first person to talk about this issue, but the idea that space, or spaces, is the product of a community, as much as it is the product of a designer, is an exciting idea and one that leaves building itself much more open to future use (and transformation).

What happens to the bodies of those who imprison queer subjectivities within a space or dwelling? If phallocentric occupations of space are related to a disavowal on the part of men of their own bodies, projected onto space in a paranoid way, what is the relation between heterocentric occupations of space and its embodiments?

There is already a metaphor for the heterocentric containment of gayness: the closet (significantly, this is also an architectural metaphor). The interesting thing about the closet, which allows me to question the word *imprison* in your question, is that the closet is *both* a prison and a safe space. This is its appeal both for the gay community and heterocentric social structure. The closet allows people to not be seen as gay but to feel safe as gay. I think that women, or gays, or other minorities, aren't "imprisoned" in or by space, because space (unless we are talking about a literal prison) is never fixed or contained, and thus is always open to various uses in the future. Men cannot literally contain women in prisons, nor do heterosexuals contain homosexuals (although perhaps they'd like to think so), because space is open to how people live it. Space is the ongoing possibility of a different inhabitation. The more one disinvests one's own body from that space, the less able one is to effectively inhabit that space as one's own. What gay communities have done is to invent a very large closet, enclosing a whole nightlife scene, a bar scene, probably a whole capitalist, consumer scene as well, as spaces of both heterocentric containment and gay freedom. Gay areas like Oxford Street in Sydney or the Castro in San Francisco are ghettos, but the interesting thing about a ghetto is that it is both the space that the dominant group has contained and the space for a generation of subcultures. This is my long and roundabout way of getting to your question about the body of the heterocentric community. These spaces are precisely the spaces inhabited and defined by sexual pleasure. The gay community, nightclubs, gay-oriented shops and cafes, offer a different, more explicitly sexualized and eroticized use of space—a space paved with images and representations produced by and for that community that helps to make clear and explicit the disavowal of a certain sexual pleasure in the heterosexual community. This sense of the erotic potential of spaces is partly what is being celebrated in the gay community.

Is this happening in a projective way?

I think what the heterosexual community projects is a disavowal of pleasure that gay bars and other such spaces represent. It is able to utilize such pleasure only vicariously, which may be why there's been such a fight over the accessibility to events at the gay Mardi Gras—debates about whether straights are allowed to go or not, and who counts as straight and who counts as gay, have threatened to tear apart the gay community itself. The significant thing, though, is that a large number of heterosexuals are attracted to these spaces and want admission or access to their ambiance. They want to go to gay bars, not just to bash gay people but to get some of the sexual vibration from the place. This is not a disavowal of "the male body" but a disavowal of the erotic potential of every body. What makes it precisely a community is the fact that, as a collective or self-identified group, it chooses sexual pleasure over conformity.

Do you think that Derrida's ready or easy incorporation into architectural discourse, which you say seems surprising because his interest appears so philosophical, so textually based and hermetically self-contained, might in fact be due to its status as philosophy—as opposed to the perhaps more overtly forceful and activist Deleuzian conception of thought?

I wouldn't say that Derrida is a theorist and Deleuze an activist. This is a mistaken understanding of the relationship of philosophy to criticism. They are both philosophers, equally "philosophical" and yet strongly political in their approaches. This is probably why their work has at different times appealed to architectural theorists. Architects and theorists of architecture simply came to Derrida before they came to Deleuze (as did literary theorists, cultural theorists, and philosophers in the Anglophone world). I do not believe that Derrida's status in architecture is all that different from Deleuze's. The main distinction seems to be that Derrida's work has appealed to architects for a little longer than Deleuze's. But this appeal is currently in the process of shifting, which may or may not be a good thing. There are an increasing number of people in architecture who are already beginning to be interested in Deleuze. My feeling is that we're going to see the same popularization of Deleuze's work as we saw for Derrida's, not only in the field of architecture but also within philosophy and the humanities more generally. It's only a question of time.

If a Deleuzian assimilation is on the horizon, though, what is to stop it from becoming reactive?

Sadly, nothing. There's nothing to stop any position from becoming reactive when it's used without thought, when it's used in an automatic or doxical way. You can be sure that the moment a theoretical position becomes popularized, explained, analyzed, and assessed with an intense scrutiny, the bulk of its practitioners begin to respond to it in automatic and routine ways. The work becomes formulaic and predictable. It seems to me that you can take any figure from the history of philosophy and make some connection with architectural theory. Anyone can be useful for rethinking habitual connections. But the moment people believe this position provides *the* truth or *the* answer, with their commentaries, dissertations, and endless analyses, then the initial thought becomes routinized, rendering it once again habitual and institutionally assimilable. I can see the potential for this kind of routinization of Deleuze, not only in architecture but elsewhere (especially in philosophy); his philosophies becoming accepted as the "next thing," the newest craze, a biblical cult filled with adoring disciples. Deleuze is no more immune to this kind of recuperation than anyone else.

Given the sort of trajectory you've just outlined, can you think of a way that philosophy spreads through the humanities and on into architecture, or of any more potentially subversive ways for Deleuze to be taken up in those areas?

Deleuze points to really interesting questions about technology. For example, his writings on virtuality have a certain resonance with the field of architecture, which is interested not just in technological incorporation but also in the openness of building to futurity or virtuality. Not simply virtual technologies but virtual buildings.

Can you quickly outline that openness?

Only in the broadest terms. This work may involve focusing on Deleuze's reading of Bergson's conception of virtuality. Bergson draws a distinction between the virtual and the possible. The possible is an already preformed version of the real. The transition from the possible to the real is a predictable one, not involving anything new or unexpected. The relationship between the virtual and the actual is one of surprise, for the virtual promises something different to the actual that it produces, and always contains in it the potential for something other than the actual. Bergson is in effect a theorist of virtuality, of the openness of the future to what befalls it. This idea could be highly productive for architecture, a discipline primarily concerned with space. Architecture considers time as historical time, or past time, but it has never really thought a concept of futurity.

In architecture, the idea of the virtual, purely in technological terms, is typically removed from its potentiality. The discipline intercedes (largely on the grounds of economy) in forcing it back into the actual.

The virtual encompasses much more than the technological: indeed, it is the condition of the possibility of technology. It is the very condition of life, and historical development, the very milieu of technological development. This is something that has been developed in the recent writings of Paul Virilio and John Rajchman within the sphere of architectural discourse.

When you say that architectural thinking needs to be confronted with thought, in the Deleuzian sense, from the outside, could it also be said that in essence the outside of architecture is the lived and gendered body?

Interesting question . . .

Perhaps architecture does take thought, in that sense, into account, but what it doesn't take into account is embodiment.

It is not that architecture excludes embodiment. Of all the arts, architecture offers embodiment the greatest sense of acceptance. But what is not embodied is the idea of sexual difference. For example, Le Corbusier spoke about Modulor Man as a gendered construct, but in a way that's not recognized even now. Architecture is a discipline, not unlike medicine, that does not need to bring the body back to itself because it's already there, albeit shrouded in latency or virtuality. Bodies are absent in architecture, but they remain architecture's unspoken condition. This is of course not only a problem for architecture but for every discipline.

The sexualized and racialized nature of embodiment, though, is something that still needs to be thought out in architectural terms. Most architectural theorists today are prepared to accept that the discipline is male dominated. But the solution to this problem is not simply to bring in more women architects (although this may be a start), but rather to rethink the very terms of the discipline in light of its foreclosure of the question of sexual difference—that is, to see the discipline as phallocentric in its structure. Architecture, however, is more open to conceptions of embodiment than many other disciplines, which is perhaps why it has actively sought to open itself to deconstructive and nomadic interventions encouraged by the work of Derrida, Foucault, and others. Traces of the body are always there in architecture.

But in a sense, these also elide a feeling of responsibility, because architecture can claim to be already dealing with the body.

To merely say that there is a body is not yet to deal with it. Bodies are there in a way that architects don't want, or can't afford, to recognize. But the body is there in an incontrovertible way. The point is to affirm that it's there, and to find the right kind of terms and values by which to make it profitable for architecture to think its own in investments in corporeality.

Do you have any suggestions as to what they might be?

This is a question that is once again about the discipline of architecture and is one that women architects, those working within the discipline, would be in a much better position to answer. I know there is a lot of work going on around the question of sexual embodiment and architecture, anthologized in *The Architect and Her Practice*, published in 1996 by the MIT Press. It is a beginning for architectural explorations of sexual embodiment and should not be too readily preempted.

The next question is actually one you yourself raised in the past. Can a Darwinian theory of evolution be applied to inanimate objects, i.e., the evolution of technology and information technology in particular?

This issue is not unrelated to the work of Deleuze and Bergson. Bergson talks about duration being a phenomenon of life, of animation. Becoming, and openness to the future, and thus evolution, are unique properties of what is alive. And yet if one is consistent with evolutionary theory, one of the main presumptions is the emergence of life from nonlife. If Bergson is prepared to grant becoming to life, using evolutionary theory to think that becoming, then it is difficult to see how he avoids granting the avenues of becoming, and thus autonomous development, to the inorganic or the chemical. This step assumes there is the possibility of thinking all sorts of inorganic forces and processes in terms of becoming. Not only what man makes—i.e., technology and culture—but also, what makes man—i.e., nature. To think becoming, in the sphere of nature as much as in the sphere of technology, seems to me a crucial project for the future.

Virilio once said, "We have the possibility of the colonization of the body by technology, as if we had the city in the body and not the city around the body." Do you have any thoughts on the idea of a technological city within the body?

I read in the newspaper a couple of days ago an extraordinary little story about a group of scientists and technicians who had devised a computer system to enable certain types of blind people to see, by way of tiny little cameras hooked up to a computer chip in the brain. They haven't succeeded in a working model yet, but they now believe that the technology is available to make it work. This is interesting because what is produced is not a body in a city but really a miniature city in the body. Miniaturized within a computer chip is already a whole set of cultural norms, values, and spaces.

It's interesting that vision is the first of the senses to be researched in this way.

I think that vision is the easiest in many ways, partly due to the history of the photographic still and then the movie camera. Because of the scopic nature of culture in general, it is not surprising that the visual is the privileged domain of the computer. Bionic ears have been around for a relatively long period of time, as internalized transistors implanted into the ear. These cameras are the visual equivalent of bionic ears. So in a way it's not the city itself but culture that is compressed into the chip in the brain, and in this sense the city is in the subject as much as surrounding it.

When we are hooked up to our computer terminals, talking to each other virtually, in different locations, the city is working through us rather than between us. Where I disagree with Virilio is that the city works through us as much as around us. The mail—the physical letter and electronic media—functions virtually. The invention of electronically generated media does not introduce us for the first time to virtuality but rather renders virtuality more graphic. We were already in a certain mode of virtuality when we wrote letters or when we painted and read. The city has never been just anything but an ongoing site of virtuality.

The body can harness a whole load of technological input, but there is a limit to its capacity for technological transformation. I don't know what this limit is, but there is a boundary beyond which the body ceases to be a body. This point is the limit of the viability of technology.

When exactly would a body cease to be a body?

It is arbitrary, but there is a certain point at which the replacement of every organ by a prosthetic one produces something fundamentally different in type. There's a point at which you can replace toenails or a spleen or whatever, and yet the body can still be considered the same. I don't know what that point is, partly because such technology still remains largely speculative or fictional. But there is a point beyond which things start to function differently—not necessarily worse, but differently. We would then have different kinds of bodies and different kinds of body functioning, and perhaps even the possibility of different becomings.

Would you become a different kind of person?

You would have to be a fundamentally different kind of person. What kind of person that is, I don't know—these kinds of imaginings are the principal preoccupation of science fiction writers.

Have you any idea as to what the implications of your writings about bodies and built space are on the recent trend of cyber-utopian writings, which seem based on the premise of liberation through a liberation from real space?

I get as much pleasure as anyone from this technology and its potentialities, but it seems to me that what this technology offers is precisely an enhancement of the body, not its replacement. The body you have is still the one sitting there hooked up to the machine, regardless of the clothing or apparatus you put on it—the information glove is still designed for the human hand. So I understand the appeal of this technology, beyond the body, dominant in cyberspace, but it seems to me to be just unthought-out or fanciful. There can be no liberation from the body, or from space, or the real. They all have a nasty habit of recurring with great insistence, however much we try to fantasize their disappearance. The cybernetic focus on the body is precisely a mode of singling out and intensifying certain regions of the body, its stimulation to maximal degrees.

You have written that the idea of leaving behind the body is a male fantasy of autogenesis. Is it also a male fantasy of complete control?

It's not just a male fantasy. I think that women have it too.

But on what basis do you think women can claim cyberspace as women's space, outside of the paradigm of autogenesis or total control?

This is an interesting question. While some think of cyberspace as a world of their own, which is the fantasy of autogenesis, a sort of Frankenstein fantasy of building a body or an entire world, many women working in cyberspace—producing art or writing—have never had that fantasy. What they see instead is that computer technology provides a space, an opportunity, a promise, of the possibility of working and producing differently. It is an incredibly effective tool—something that speeds everything up, makes it look shiny, gives it a polished look, yet it also transforms how we can work. This is quite different from (and considerably more modest than) the idea of its producing another world, or the simulation of this world. This is nothing but a fantasy of self-mastery and self-containment that is unattainable elsewhere. Many women have a primarily pragmatic relation to these technologies and refuse to be mesmerized and seduced by their phantasmatic promise. It is an immensely seductive technology, but part of this seduction is not its ability to transcend this world so much as the allure or the pleasure of its use. For example, like many people, I have a powerful attachment to my Macintosh. It's about the beauty of the design, the ease with which it allows you to do certain things, and its capacity to transform how we think what we do. Much of the appeal that cyberspace holds for those of us outside the field of fiction is simply practical: the technology enables us to do interesting things quickly and simply. There is a pleasure in its efficiency. The more pragmatic our relation to these technologies, the more we will enjoy them.

This attachment to the machine or computer is, of course, not unlike the relation of the user to drugs—one can use drugs to build up a fantasy of a complete existence safe from the rest of the world. But drugs needn't be seen that way. Drugs can rather be interpreted as another form of technology, as a mode of corporeal or conceptual enhancement or intensification that doesn't aim or hope to build a world, as an alternative to the real. Technology isn't inherently masculine or phallocentric or ethnocentric, although certainly its modes of production and circulation are closely invested in power relations. But in spite of this, it holds a certain promise: it can be used in all sorts of ways with all sorts of aims or goals in mind. It is both the condition of power and a possibility for its subversion, depending on how it is used, by whom, and with what effects.

So like drugs, technology can also be addictive?

No question about it. Technology *is* addictive. Whenever any mainframe goes down, people go berserk, deprived momentarily of their hit of daily e-mail. Perhaps it is not so bad as that, but there is a broad resemblance. They are both bound up in the metaphors of addiction.

Virilio has written that interactivity is to real space what radioactivity is to the atmosphere—a pollution. This again seems to complicate and undermine the claims of those who want to use cyberspace as a utopian space in which phallocentric thought can be subverted.

There are no utopian spaces anywhere except in the imagination. But this absence doesn't necessarily have to be restrictive. If we had a utopian space, we would already be there, and yet the phallocentric world would continue intervening within it, for it would be a space alongside of, rather than contesting, the space of the real. It is to our benefit that we cannot access this space because it means that we must continue to fight in the real, in the spaces we occupy now. We must fight for results we can't foresee and certainly can't guarantee.

You have used in the past Roger Caillois's construction of psychasthenia—a depersonalization by assimilation to space.[1] Do you think that in the postmodern city this is our general experience of space—especially in terms of the media bombardment of commercial spaces like shopping centers, the kind of artificial spaces that in some ways coax us into lapses of identity, or some kind of out-of-body experience?

There is a certain joy in our immersion in space. It is important to recognize that you can attain a certain (temporary) depersonalization and still enjoy it, enjoy the expansion and permeability of bodily boundaries. Are you asking whether the modern city, the postmodern city, is alienating? If so, my answer has to be, no. The spaces of the mall, ironically, are for many people precisely the spaces of the most intense pleasure. It is not simply the pleasure of consumption and acquisition (the pleasure of shopping), but also a certain pleasure in the spectacle and community interactions, even of the most commercial kinds. There is, of course, also the pleasure of the *flâneur*, of strolling and observing, of seeing and being seen, of browsing amongst objects and people simultaneously. Some people hate malls, but for all the people that hate them there are many, particularly the young, who are drawn to them, finding within their spaces a highly conducive milieu. The mall has become a certain condition or way of shopping that we can make highly pleasurable.

Do you see a relation of psychasthenia to virtual space?

There is a possible relationship but not a necessary one. We can have each without the other. Psychasthenia occurs when the boundaries of personal identity are collapsed and the subject is no longer able to distinguish what is inside from what is outside, what is self and what is other. It is clearly a very disturbing and debilitating psychical disorder. Cyberspace does not in itself induce psychosis or psychasthenia: one requires a certain bodily and conceptual cohesion to even enter cyberspace with all its apparatus and equipment. Indeed, there is a certain safety in entertaining one's fantasies and hopes in cyberspace precisely because it is virtual, not actual. This is one of the pleasures of cyberspace: you may have the possibility of at least temporarily disturbing an identity. Whether this disturbance becomes psychasthenic is perhaps another question. I think the fantasy is that you just get another identity different from your own; waiting a while to use it, like donning a new outfit, is part of the allure of cyberspace.

This is a similar fantasy to the idea of the mall as a space in which you can shop around for another identity.

But you can't. At the mall, all you can do is use its social spaces, including cyberspace, as supplementary augmentations of aspects of your identity. This is perhaps a minor augmentation, not really as radical as some proponents of virtual identity might claim. You don't become a woman by adopting a female identity in cyberspace if you are a man in real space. Cyberspace has been seen as the site of a certain cross-dressing, or swapping of identities, that can only be phantasmatic and supplementary. But while entering cyberspace does not make the man a woman, it may make him see other possibilities for being a man.

How would this inability to change identity at will relate back to the idea of a totally technologized body? It's the old watch analogy—if you change the face of a watch and then change its wrist strap, do you have the same watch? Similarly, if you change your toenails and then also change x, y, and z, are you the same person? If you were able to change all of these things at will, would you also be changing your identity?

No. It's you that's making the change, and it's you that is your identity. If you think you're changing, the you that does the changing hasn't in fact changed at all: it remains a sovereign agent, a reigning consciousness. Your identity is changing all of the time, but it's you who is being changed rather than you who is the agent of that change. We are effects more than causes. You can choose what clothes to wear but you can't change the you that's wearing them. The very notion of choice is bound up with your identity.

I think this is the fantasy that is behind certain queer politics—the idea that you can choose your sexual identity. I suspect it stems from a misreading of Judith Butler's work on performativity: that you can just perform what you want to be. The problem is that if you choose to perform a certain sexual identity, then you have not changed at all by undertaking that identity, you're just acting out. It would be nice to be able to choose an identity, but in fact it is chosen for us. Our agency comes from how we accept that designated position, and the degree to which we refuse it, the way we live it out.

You write about the relationship between bodies and cities as being a mutual one in that each imbricates the other—how we embody virtual space and it, us. How does this mutually imbricating relationship work, given that virtual space seems to privilege sight over other corporeal experiences?

The fact that cyberspace is primarily visual is not a particular problem in itself. We were all already completely visually immersed, even before the advent of cyberspace. Cyberspace has become embodied in the screen not accidentally or contingently but because of the visualized nature of our culture and its prevailing pleasures. The technology predicated on an economy of watching has been pervasive for at least a century. In our culture television has captured our imagination through the eye. The fact that computer technology has become embodied in a screen-type technology, rather than as some other form, is an interesting historical question, but it isn't really simply about a momentary technological privileging of the visual.

If cybertechnology is able to gain a grip on bodies and their desires, it is because the virtual or the cyber is also always already an integral element in the subject before its introduction to this particular kind of technology. For us as bounded, unified, cohesive subjects, subjects who have entered and passed through Lacan's mirror stage, we enter the world of the virtual through the mirror which gives us a sense of who we are. An external image presents us with an image of ourselves. This is the structure of identification: I make myself like the image of myself. It is this allure of the image, so primordial in our infantile development that a child prefers to see an image of a bird rather than a real bird, that partly explains the irresistible hold that television has for us. The self-representations of cyberspace are appealing insofar as they reproduce and promise even more narcissistic satisfaction than the television screen. It is also no accident that the integration of the television into the computer screen is the easiest and most direct development ahead of us in technological progress.

In both your work and that of Luce Irigaray, the idea of chora seems to be central to the way in which feminists think about place and space and dwelling. Could this concept also apply itself to a terminal dwelling? And by "terminal" I mean the computer screen, the space of the screen.

This can't be your only space. This computerized or virtual space is always housed inside another space—the space of bodily dwelling. You can't be in a computer space unless you're also in another space. This is why it's always only augmentational. You cannot set up your terminal outside real space because, even outdoors, it is always housed in real space. You're already doing it in your house, or in your office, which means that the whole structure of *chora* still applies, even in the fantasy that cyberspace is somehow beyond or transcendent of real space. You can't escape the building to get into cyberspace, you've got to go through the building to get into cyberspace.

In your essay "Women, Chora, Dwelling," you wrote that the future project for women was to begin to rethink space and to reoccupy it as their own.[2] *Since the writing of that essay, have you seen evidence of the sorts of ways in which those new modes of inhabiting have taken shape or how they could work?*

I don't really know how to respond to that. I guess the short answer is, no, I haven't thought about it, and I'm not sure that looking at empirical projects involving women architects is really the way to answer the question of how to rethink the relations between women and space.

But in terms of what we talked about earlier—the cyberfeminists' occupation of space—do you think that a group of feminists could take something like your idea of chora and the idea of women occupying space literally, even though, as you've said, these spaces are only a projection from within an existing space?

Cyberfeminists are trying to occupy space, virtual space, differently now, and I think that this is good. But if we're talking about actual buildings, then a really complicated problem is raised: there has never been a space by and for women. Even women-only spaces (feminist or lesbian spaces) are ones set up in reaction or opposition to patriarchal cultural space. Both today and in the recent past, to produce a women-only space is to produce that space as separatist and thus as reactive to the dominant male culture. I no longer think that this is a viable strategy. Other than something like a separatist reclaiming of spaces as women, it's not clear to me how women can or do occupy space. We need quite different terms by which to understand space and spatiality, if we are to be able to more successfully rethink the relations between women and space. We would also have to consider very carefully the boundaries of what constitutes the occupation of space and occupying it "as a woman." This, in turn, raises all sorts of political questions. If you are a woman architect, you may have better resources than I have to think about occupying space quite differently and outside of the terms of separatist refusal.

In what sorts of ways will you continue to work on feminisms and the body?

The best way to answer that question is indirectly. Personally, I had to leave feminism and the body in order to come at it a different way. It's just not appealing at the moment, partly because I've worked myself to death in this area and I need to reinvent an approach to it. I had considered another big project that didn't have anything to do with either feminism or the body but which dealt with some of the questions raised in my earlier work in a much more indirect way. I am interested, for example, in questions about materiality—the nature of atoms, and more general issues of historical and evolutionary becoming. How I can develop these ideas in feminist terms, I don't know. But I feel sure that in order to keep my feminist work alive I have to keep it at bay, at a bit of a distance. In short, it is unclear to me where my new work is going. Perhaps you should ask again in a year or two.

Do you feel as though feminisms and the body—the idea of embodied subjectivity—has been done and that we should take it as said?

No. But my comments about Deleuze can also apply here. There is still a lot of work to be done on the body and the implications of the body for knowledge; on the other hand, it is now such a popular topic—everybody's talking about it and in the main it's done in a routine fashion. The question then is really how to make it fresh again, how to make it incisive. I first started dealing with the body in 1981 at a time when it was still shocking to think about the body, because everyone was interested in the mind (in terms of either consciousness, the unconscious, or ideology). It is not shocking anymore; it is respected, and indeed the expected thing to do. For me the interesting thing is to try to do something unexpected or something still fresh and incisive.

Of course, the body is not a topic without value. It is still of tremendous importance, but it has to be done carefully—though in a nonroutine way. The moment that it becomes routine and taken for granted—which is its status at the moment within feminist theory—then we need to think about it again and perhaps come at it, or something else, differently.

How would you characterize this different approach? In a Deleuzian way? Or are you abandoning it entirely?

It's not a question of abandonment. I don't think that one ever drops what one has been through. You always carry it with you. I don't want to embark next on a big Deleuzian project. I've incorporated what I need from Deleuze and I want to do something else. I don't know if there's one way forward; it depends on what projects you're looking at and the interests one has. For a while, in feminist theory, everyone wanted broadly the same sort of thing. Now it's no longer clear to me that that's a good thing for feminism as a whole. A proliferation of lots of different kinds of projects would be much more interesting and should be accommodated within the parameters of feminist theory.

Spivak has written that she cannot think of the body and that the body cannot be thought—that she cannot approach it. What do you think she means by that?

It is true that one cannot think the body because we still don't know what the body is, or what it is capable of doing, what its limits or its capacities are. More than that, we don't know what a body is because a body is always in excess of our knowing it, and provides the ongoing possibility of thinking or otherwise knowing it. It is always in excess of any representation, and indeed, of all representations. This is part of Deleuze's point: that we don't know what a body can do, for the body is the outside of thought, which doesn't mean that it is unthinkable but that we approach it in thought without fully grasping it. But I don't know if that's what Spivak meant.

This ignorance is also pervasive even if we look at the life sciences and those specifically devoted to an analysis of the body. Medical science doesn't really understand the body: the very discipline devoted to the body doesn't understand it, let alone any of the other disciplines less specifically focused on it.

Would you say then that medicine still treats the body in a mechanistic, Cartesian way?

That would be to oversimplify it a little. The medical profession is not simply made up of backward philosophers. Typically, the body is treated mechanically, but this need not be a problem. There are, however, many other more complicated approaches developed within contemporary medicine which go a long way toward problematizing any vestiges of Cartesianism (many of the most convincing refutations of Cartesian thought come from neuroscience). There are many extremely interesting projects going on within medicine at the moment that may have broad implications for thinking about minds and bodies in different terms: projects within neurology, endocrinology, genetics, and immunology, among many others, which are much more sophisticated than any Cartesian framework. We in the humanities should be much more open to reading that work instead of simply dismissing it with hostility. We should be reading medical texts, not simply because they may or may not be self-informative, but also because these discourses help produce the kinds of bodies and subjectivities we will be destined to live out (as we age, grow ill, move toward death, and so on). We should be thinking more about these ideas—what is the latest research? what do we make of it?—rather than immediately arguing for its dismissal.

There is much that is interesting in the tropes and metaphors of illness, invasion, contamination that abound in the medical literature beyond case studies. These metaphors are significant not just because they provide a rhetoric of medical intervention but also because medical discourses and practices are historically privileged in helping form and produce bodies and subjects. The way disease is conceptualized is both borrowed from and at the same time feeds into cultural and social life. Medicine is of course not the only body of discourse to make such social projections and introjections explicit. This is true of all the institutionally sanctioned disciplinary forces and discourses. Much the same could be said of the law. Or architecture.

This is an essay on "outer space." The "outer spaces" I would like to address here are not those explored by the astronaut (such spaces at the moment are still understood only in terms of an extension of terrestrial spatiality) but those spaces at the limit of reason itself, those spaces occupied by the infant, the psychotic, the computer hacker, the dreamer, and the visionary: cultural outer spaces.

Two Lived Spatiality (The Spaces of Corporeal Desire)

I have been working on a project of rethinking bodies for several years now that involves seeing the body as a, indeed, as *the*, primary sociocultural product. It involves a double displacement, an alteration or realignment of a number of conceptual schemas that have thus far been used to think bodies: on the one hand, it involves problematizing a whole series of binary oppositions and dichotomous categories governing the ways we understand bodies, their relations to other objects and to the world (among the more crucial oppositions challenged by reconceptualizing the terms in which bodies are thought are the distinctions between mind and body, subject and object, psychological and biological, gender and sex, culture and nature, etc.). This is no easy task: it may in fact prove impossible to definitively rid ourselves of binary categorizations, given that our language, all of our concepts, and the intellectual frameworks we use to think them are derived from a vast history of dichotomous thinking that we have inherited. On the other hand, my project also involves displacing the privileges accorded to mind, to consciousness, or to the psyche over the body and materiality: it involves understanding the interaction of the social and the individual in terms of the production and inscription of bodily surfaces, as the constitution of concretely particular, socially determinate modes of corporeality. Instead of seeing the body as a surface or shell that houses a depth or interiority, I have been interested in exploring subjectivity and the inevitably related question of sexual difference, in terms of the complexities, specificities, and materialities of bodies *alone*. This project is based on a risky wager: that all the effects of depth, of interiority, of the inside, all the effects of consciousness (and the unconscious), can be thought in terms of corporeal surfaces, in terms of the rotations, convolutions, inflections, and torsions of the body itself. My wager is to think the subject in terms of the rotation of impossible shapes in illegible spaces (my favorite example at the moment is the Möbius strip).

Conceptions of space and time are necessary coordinates of a reinterrogation of the limits of corporeality: there are always two mutually defining and interimplicating sets of terms, always defined in necessarily reciprocal terms, because any understanding of bodies requires a spatial and temporal framework. Conversely, space and time themselves remain conceivable insofar as they become accessible for us corporeally. I would contend that space and time are not, as Kant suggests, a priori mental or conceptual categories that precondition and make possible our concepts; rather, they are a priori *corporeal* categories, whose precise features and idiosyncrasies parallel the cultural and historical specificities of bodies. Indeed, it might be convincingly argued that there is a correlation of historically specific conceptions of subjectivity, spatiality, and temporality. The Ptolemaic space-time framework is isomorphic with the prevailing concept of the hierarchically positioned subject, the power structure of master and slave; the Galilean universe could be seen as congruent with the Cartesian concept of the self-given and autonomous subject; the Einsteinian universe in its turn may be correlated with the psychoanalytic fissuring of the subject; and virtual spaces may be correlations of the postmodern subject. The limits of possible spaces are the limits of possible modes of corporeality: the body's infinite pliability is a measure of the infinite plasticity of the spatiotemporal universe in which it is housed and through which bodies become real, are lived, and have effects.

1. The Space-Time of Lived Bodies

I will not attempt here to present either a detailed or a very convincing outline of psychoanalytic concepts of subjectivity and spatiality, which link the sense of psychical integrity (provided through the genesis of the ego), the development of a sense of bodily integrity and cohesion, and the acquisition of a stable spatiotemporal framework to the development of sexual difference, but rather will provide a broad, general outline of some of the ingredients necessary for such an account. I will concentrate only on what can be called the formation of the "body image" or "body phantom," a neuropsychological mapping of the body, not in the terms provided by biology but in terms of the psychical significance of the body.

Freud claims that the form of the ego is provided through a psychical mapping or libidinal tracing of the erotogenicity of the body. The ego is not a self-contained entity or thing so much as a bodily tracing, a cartography of the erotogenic intensity of the senses and organs, a kind of internalized image of the degrees of the intensity of sensations in the child's body. Freud here enigmatically refers to the "cortical homunculus," a much-beloved idea in nineteenth-century neurology (one to which Lacan also makes curious reference):

The ego is first and foremost a bodily ego: it is not merely a surface entity, but is itself the projection of a surface. If we wish, [we
can] identify it with the "cortical homunculus" of the anatomists,
which stands on its head in the cortex, sticks up its heels, faces
backwards, and as we know, has its speech-area on the left hand
side.[1]

Freud regards the processes of psychical integration as
parallel to and bound up with physiological development.
The ego is a kind of meeting point between the social and
the corporeal, the site through which the body is produced
as a determinate type according to the requirements of
culture. It is in turn one of the sites of social resistance and
transcription of the social by the corporeal. Lacan, relying
as he does on Freud, also regards the ego as a projection of
the significance of the body for the subject, its representation through the image of others (including its own reflection in a mirror). Lacan refers primarily to an "imaginary
body," an internalized image of the meaning that the body
has for the subject, for others, and for the sociosymbolic
order. It is an individual and collective fantasy of the body's
forms and possibilities of action and signification. Only
the presumption of such an imaginary anatomy, Lacan
claims, can explain the peculiar nonorganic connections
formed in hysteria, the existence of the phantom limb, and
the various spatial disorders of the psychotic. The imaginary anatomy reflects individual, familial, and social be-
liefs about the body rather than an awareness of its
biological "nature":

The imaginary anatomy . . . varies with the ideas (clear or confused) about bodily functions which are prevalent in a given culture. It all happens as if the body-image had an autonomous
existence of its own and by autonomous I mean here independent
of objective structure.[2]

Hysteria (e.g., in anorexia), the phantom limb, hypo-chondria, and indeed, sexuality itself, testify to the pliability or fluidity of what is usually considered the inert, fixed, passive, biological body. If it exists at all (and it is no longer clear to me that it does), the biological body exists for the subject only through the mediation of a series of images or representations of the body and its capacities for movement and action. The body phantom or döppelganger, the most frightening of themes in the horror genre (brilliantly represented cinematically by *Dead Ringers* and *The Krays*, and a very regular motif in horror television, from *The Twilight Zone* onward), is also the condition of the capacity for undertaking voluntary action. This may explain the visceral horror of one's own self-image stealing one's identity.

The body phantom is the condition of the subject's capacity not only to adapt to but also to become integrated with various objects, instruments, tools, and machines. It is the condition of the body's inherent openness and pliability to and in its social context. As Paul Schilder, one of the pioneers of the body-image, has made clear, it is the capacity to integrate or internalize otherwise apparently external objects into one's own corporeal activities that enables the blind person to feel through a cane, or allows the driver of a car, or even a pilot, to be able to accurately judge distances relative to the car or plane (no matter how large). It is the condition that enables us to acquire and use prosthetic devices, glasses, contact lenses, artificial limbs, surgical implants in place of our sense organs; and it is the condition of our capacity, in sensual experiences, to bodily incorporate the objects of our desire through sustained intimate contact. The body phantom is the link between our biological and cultural existence, between our "inner" psyche and our "external" body, that which enables a passage or a transformation from one to the other. Moreover, it is the body image that enables the human body to shift its various significances: to endow one part of the body with the meaning and value of another; to displace sexuality from genitals to other zones, or vice versa; to become infinitely malleable, transposable, mobile—enabling, for example, the whole of the body to take on phallic significance.

The pliability of the body image, its capacity to take on other significances, is admirably attested to by the hypermasculine inversion into femininity of the steroid user, the bodybuilder (a wonderful, paradoxical term), the man who, in conforming to a hypervirility, chemically shrinks the penis in the process. Arnold Schwarzenegger is quite explicit in saying that the hard body for which he and others strive is an orgasmic body, a thoroughly sexualized body, infused with libidinal significance in every gland, blood vessel, and muscular grouping, a body that takes on the function of the phallus. In Freudian terms, the feminine equivalent of this masculine investment of phallic significance in the whole of the female body is called narcissism (an investment in a part rather than the whole of the female body is precisely what constitutes hysterical conversion—this makes bodybuilding both narcissistic and hysterical!). In an interview on the BBC's five-part series *Naked Hollywood*, Schwarzenegger confesses, "Pumping iron is like having sex. Can you believe how much I am in Heaven? I am, like, *coming* day and night." It is the whole body coming. This is only possible because the plasticity of the body image enables any or all parts of the body to acquire or transform the meaning that first constituted them. The steroid body attests to the literality of the body as infinitely pliable and to its necessarily mobile representational or significational status.

2. Psychotic or Insect Space

I have already suggested that notions of the body always imply, and in turn produce, notions of spatiality. Now I would like to make a slight detour into the world of insect spatiality, which may provide an index to understanding the peculiar psychical dislocation that characterizes many forms of psychosis, the most outer kind of space in psychical functioning. Here I want to turn briefly to the pioneering work of Roger Caillois, who, in his paper "Mimicry and Legendary Psychasthenia" (1935), explores the spatiality of the phenomenon of mimicry in the natural world. Mimesis is particularly significant in outlining the ways in which the relations between an organism and its environment are blurred and confused, the way in which its environment is not an external feature of the insect's life but is constitutive of its "identity." In opposition to the dominant, adaptationist view, Caillois claims that mimicry in the insect world does not have clear survival value: its purpose is not to ensure the survival of the species through providing camouflage against its predators. Mimicry has little survival value, he points out, for most predators rely on a sense of smell rather than on the visual elements required for homeomorphic disguise.

Caillois considers mimicry to be a "dangerous luxury," an excess over nature, a superabundance inexplicable in terms of the species' survival:

We are thus dealing with a *luxury* and even a dangerous luxury, for there are cases in which mimicry causes the creature to go from bad to worse: geometer-moth caterpillars simulate shoots of shrubbery so well that gardeners cut them with their pruning shears. The case of the Phyllia is even sadder: they browse among themselves, taking each other for real leaves, in such a way that one might accept the idea of a sort of collective masochism leading to mutual homophagy, the simulation of the leaf being a *provocation* to cannibalism in this kind of totem feast.[3]

The mimicry characteristic of certain species has to do with the distinction it makes between itself and its environment, including other species. Mimicry is not a consequence of space but rather of the *representation* of space, the way space is perceived by the insect and its predators. Caillois likens the insect's ability for morphological mimicry to a psychosis that Pierre Janet described as "legendary psychasthenia," a psychosis in which the subject is unable to locate himself or herself in a position in space:

It is with represented space that the drama becomes specific since the living creature, the organism, is no longer the origin of the co-ordinates, but one point among others; it is dispossessed of its privilege and literally *no longer knows where to place itself.* One can indeed recognize the characteristic scientific attitude and, indeed, it is remarkable that represented spaces are just what is multiplied by contemporary science: Finsler's spaces, Fermat's spaces, Riemann-Christoffel's hyper-space [we may add here too the space of virtual realities], abstract, generalized, open and closed spaces, spaces dense in themselves, thinned out and so on. The feeling of personality, considered as the organism's feeling of distinctness from its surroundings, of the connection between consciousness and a particular point in space, cannot fail under these conditions to be seriously undermined; one then enters into the psychology of psychasthenia.[4]

Psychasthenia is a response to the lure posed by space for subjectivity. The subject can take up a position only by being able to situate its body in a position in space, a position from which it relates to other objects. This anchoring of subjectivity in its body is the condition of a coherent identity and, moreover, the condition under which the subject has a perspective on the world, becomes a source of perception, a point from which vision emanates. In psychasthenia, this meshing of subject and body fails to occur. The psychotic is unable to locate himself or herself where he or she should be: such subjects may look at themselves from the outside, as others would; they may hear the

voices of others inside their own heads. They are captivated and replaced, not by another subject (the horror of
the double I mentioned) but by space itself:

*I know where I am, but I do not feel as though I'm at the spot where I
find myself.* To these dispossessed souls, space seems to be a de-
vouring force. Space pursues them, encircles them, digests
them. . . . It ends by replacing them. Then the body separates itself from thought, the individual breaks the boundary of his skin
and occupies the other side of his senses. He tries to look at himself from any point whatever in space. He feels himself becoming
space, *dark space where things cannot be put.* He is similar, not similar to something, but just *similar.* And he invents spaces of which
he is the "convulsive possession."[5]

Psychosis is the human analog of mimicry in the insect world (which thus may be considered as a kind of natural psychosis?): both represent what Caillois describes as
a "depersonalization by assimilation to space."[6] The psychotic and the insect renounce their right to occupy a per-
spectival point, abandoning themselves to being located,
for themselves, as others, from the point of view of others.
The primacy of the subject's own perspective is replaced
by the gaze of another for whom the subject is merely *a*
point in space, not *the* focal point organizing space. The
representation of space is thus a correlate of one's ability to
locate oneself as the point of origin or reference of space.
Space as it is represented is a complement of the kind of
subject who occupies it. The barrier between the inside
and the outside, in the case of the human subject as much
as the insect creature, is ever permeable, suffused not only
by objects and apparatuses but by spatiality itself.
　　Psychoanalytic theory, and Caillois's contribution to
it, can be read in terms of the constitution of the subject's
sexed body through various forces of signification and

representation—the meaning the body has for others or for itself, its socioeconomic constitution as a subject, and above all the psychical, economic, and libidinal constitution of bodies as sexually differentiated—all are key ingredients in understanding the subject's embodied relations to spatiality. It is significant that neither psychoanalytic theory, nor Caillois's reworking of it, adequately acknowledge that there are always at least two irreducibly different types of body, and thus two types of subjectivity, perhaps operating within two different orders of spatiality. A whole history of theorists of the body—from Spinoza through Nietzsche, Freud, Lacan, Merleau-Ponty, Foucault, Derrida, Deleuze, Baudrillard, and others—have not acknowledged the sexual specificity of the body or the sexual specificity of knowledges, including their own, and have not recognized their own complicity in the consolidation of patriarchy, which is always at the same time a neutering and neutralization of the female sex. Psychoanalysis is notorious for the irredeemably central position it accords to the function of the phallus, a function that inevitably renders women either as the pathetic counterparts of men (in the masculinity complex) or as castrated, lacking, passive, incapable—men's opposites. We cannot know in advance what a recognition of the sexual specificity of bodies entails in the construction of theories and knowledges, cultural artifacts and social relations. But it is clear that such a recognition entails seeing all of cultural production thus far (including the production of knowledge) as production from the point of view of only one type of corporeality, one type of subject (white, male, European, middle-class). This realization, in turn, means clearing the way to create other kinds of productive spaces in which other kinds of corporeality—women's, among others—may also be able to develop their own positions, perspectives, interests, productions.

3. Virtual Space and Human Bodies

I am fascinated by the ways in which new computer technologies and virtual realities are represented: in spite of claims that they are something completely new and different, they repeat the same old presumptions about sexual neutrality, and thus the same obliterations of sexual difference that have marked science, technology, and mass communications in the West. I am not suggesting that science or technology are male dominated or inherently patriarchal and thus bad: my attitude is much more pragmatic. All cultural production is phallocentric (in that it covers over women's specificity), but this does not mean that we shouldn't use it; it just means we should use it *very carefully*, aware of the risks it might entail. I feel the same way about computer-associated technologies, with their promise of virtual realities (a promise that culminates in the idea of virtual sex, sex in which bodies and distances are rendered redundant, a sexuality that poses the apparently utopian ideal of disembodied pleasure, a pleasure—perhaps, but probably not?—transcending the phallus and the domination of the male body).

By "virtual reality" I understand a system of computer simulations of three-dimensional spaces, themselves laid out within a more generalized space, now known as cyberspace. Virtual realities are computer-generated and -fed worlds that simulate key elements of "real space" or at least its dominant representations—for example, its dimensionality, its relations of resemblance and contiguity—acting as a partial homology for a "real" space within which it is located. Rather than objects, information occupies this virtual space. Cyberspace (the space of software) is located within a "real space" (the space of hardware), although it becomes more and more difficult to definitively separate the two. A virtual space is an interactive environment in which a crucial ingredient is a subject ("wetware") located in real space (its reality, incidentally, is attested to by the psychotic as much as by the normal subject). This subject does not so much direct or control the action as vicariously participate—perhaps through some informational delegate ("the puppet")—in a virtual environment that is responsive to and constitutive of the subject's activities within it. Cyberspace is "the broad electronic net in which virtual realities are spun. Virtual reality is only one type of phenomenon within electronic space. Cyberspace, as a general medium, invites participation. In the framework of the everyday world, cyberspace is the set of orientation points by which we find our way around a bewildering amount of data."[7]

Virtual reality (VR) promises a paradoxical contact as a distance—the possibility of the interaction of one or several subjects who are spatially dispersed but who can "come together," can interact, through a computer terminal, with each other and with their shared environment. They can, in principle at least, share perceptual experiences, can even make love, though they may be separated by thousands of miles in real space. Rheingold quotes from a well-known researcher in cyberspace technology, Randall Walser, who proclaims that much of the excitement generated by VR and cyberspace has to do with the transparency, dispensability, or redundancy of the body—in other words, the capacity of computer technology to transcend the body. VR promises fulfillment of the age-old (male) fantasy of disembodied self-containment, an existence without debt, commitment, ties—the fantasy of the self-made liberal subject. This fantasy is necessarily a disavowal of femininity and maternity, and more particularly and directly, a denial of the linkage between the (sexed) body and the (sexed) subject. As Rheingold quotes Walser:

As you conduct more of your life and affairs in cyberspace your conditioned notion of a unique and immutable body will give way to a far more liberated notion of "body" as something quite disposable and, generally, limiting. You will find that some bodies work best in some situations while others work best in others. The ability to radically and compellingly change one's body-image is bound to have a deep psychological effect, calling into question just what you consider yourself to be. . . . Who, then, are you? It may seem, from your present view in physical reality, that you will be centered as you are right now, in your physical body. It always comes back to that, right? But does it, even when you spend nearly all your waking life in cyberspace, with *any body or personality you care to adopt?*[8]

The fantasy of disembodiment is that of autogenesis, a megalomaniacal attempt to provide perfect control in a world where things tend to become messy, complicated, or costly; it is a control fantasy. The idea that one could take on a second-order or virtual body and somehow leave one's real body behind with no trace or residue, with no effects or repercussions, is a luxury only afforded the male subject. That one enters cyberspace only as a disembodied mind, as neither male nor female, is a central assumption underlying the current enthusiasm surrounding VR.

Not surprisingly, this assumption is made most explicit in the much toyed-with idea of virtual sex. "Teledildonics" (a virtual sex named after the dildo, itself a replication of the representations of the erect penis) represents the fantasy (a male fantasy, though no doubt it can have its feminist variants) of a perfectly controllable, programmable quasi-prostitution. It shares the same underlying structure as pornography and prostitution: the idea of a sexual "relation" in which the body of man figures for nothing, hiding itself in the gaze it directs outward to the female body.

Teledildonics has been understood as the possibility of disembodiment rather than as an inherently sexually specific mode of corporeal interfacing. The point is that the body is not and can never be left behind. Transcendence can never occur at the expense of the body. To believe one can transcend the body is to enter a psychosis, a collective (and thus nonpathological) psychosis of male self-surpassing. I refer here to Rheingold's enthusiastic speculations, which are quite representative of, and possibly more accessible than, many others:

Picture yourself a couple of decades hence, dressed for a hot night in the virtual village. Before you climb into a suitably padded chamber and put on your 3D glasses, you slip into a lightweight (eventually, one would hope, diaphanous) body-suit, something like a body stocking, but with the kind of intimate snugness of a condom [!]. Embedded in the inner surface of the suit, using a technology that does not yet exist, is an array of intelligent sensor-effectors . . . that can receive and transmit a realistic sense of tactile presence. . . .

You can reach out your virtual hand, pick up a virtual block, and by running your fingers over the object, feel the surfaces and edges, by means of the effectors that exert counterforces against your skin. The counterforces correspond to the kinds of forces you would encounter when handling a nonvirtual object. . . . You can run your cheek over (virtual) satin, and feel the difference when you encounter (virtual) flesh. Or you can gently squeeze something soft and pliable and feel it stiffen under your touch.

. . . Your partner(s) can move independently in the cyberspace, and your representations are able to touch each other, even though your physical bodies might be continents apart. You will whisper in your partner's ear, feel your partner's breath on your neck. You will run your hands over your lover's clavicle, and 6000 miles away, an array of effectors are triggered, in just the right sequence, at just the right frequency, to convey the touch exactly the way you wish it to be conveyed. If you don't like the way the encounter is going, or someone requires your presence in physical reality, you can turn it all off by flicking a switch and taking off your virtual birthday suit.[9]

Perhaps without even knowing it, Rheingold has spilled the beans (or bytes) on what is at stake here. I have no objection, in principle, to virtual technologies, or for that matter, any technologies. My reservations come from the ways in which it is conceived and put to use, the ways in which its potentialities are severely limited, and are necessarily sexually specific without any adequate acknowledgment. What Rheingold voices here is the common fantasy of a laborless pleasure, a pleasure or desire that has no responsibilities; a work of consumption with no trace, no effect, no cost of labor, no residue—the perfect God fantasy, and a complete obliteration of all traces, of the gaps, the intervals, the remainders, of sexual difference.

To have sex but to suffer no consequences, to pay no price (bar financial), to bear no responsibility. Something for nothing. This fantasy accords perfectly with the phallicization of the male body only at the unacknowledged expense of the castration of the female body. Gay and straight men share and live a collective fantasy of the transparency and self-containment of the male body (and the corresponding opacity and dependence of the female body—its status as "eternal enigma" or "dark continent"). Men share a will or desire not to see the (cultural) otherness of the structure of desire in their corporeality relative to women's—the alienness to women of men's capacity to reify bodily organs; to be interested in organs rather than the people to whom they belong; to seek sexuality without intimacy; to strive for anonymity amidst promiscuity; to detach themselves from sexual engagement in order to establish voyeuristic distance; to enjoy witnessing violence and associate it with sexual pleasure; to see their own organs and those of others as tools, devices, or instruments of pleasure rather than as part of the body in which pleasure is distributed.

Such a sexuality would quite readily find itself at home in the production of controlled virtual spaces, spaces whose boundaries, whose frame and placement in the "real world," provide it with a barrier against seepage or drifting into the rest of life. VR offers the fantasy of a 1960s style polysexuality, with none of the nasty consequences: a high without drugs or the hangover, sex without pregnancy or disease, pleasure without the body. This is the fantasy only of a male body, the anticipation of pleasure or sex that is so corporeally self-distancing that mastery over distance itself becomes the turn-on. Just as pornography has, up to now at least, offered little if anything for women as women (whether heterosexual or lesbian)—that is, just as all pornography, whether it depicts men or women or both, is made for a male spectator—so too VR tends to become a form of self-embrace for male sexuality. (My objections to pornography are not that it is morally wrong or should be banned but that it is boring and ritualistic, and needs to be made relevant to and pleasurable for women.) Virtual spaces run the probability of only ever becoming another space that men colonize in the name of a generic humanity but that serves only their particular interests.

Given the lived spatiality of the body-subject as it psychically develops, as it is manifested in psychosis (human and natural), and as it is anticipated in incipient cyberspaces, I would argue that there is no such thing as a stable, fixed reality, a "real" space readily separable from its dysfunctional breakdowns (in psychosis) and its deceptive simulations (in cyberspace). The spaces that count as real function in collusion with and through covering over

other spaces: lived spatiality itself vacillates and transforms between sleep and awakeness; between the indeterminate multiple spaces of infancy and the hierarchized,
organized, and bounded spaces of childhood; between the
childhood space of the neighborhood and the adolescent
space of the city and the adult space of the home. Our
technological productions are themselves the products of
collective fantasies of the body's forms and functions, its
weaknesses and vulnerabilities, its points of augmentation
and supplementation, its reading of bodily zones as sites of
prosthetic transcription, a mapping and remapping of corporeal alignments and intensities. But the problem that
women, feminists, face is that the body that underlies and
frames the terms of such representations has always been
the functioning male body under the name of the neutral
human. The production of alternative models, registers,
alignments, interrelations, perspectives, and corporeali-
ties themselves, is what, among other things, is at stake in
feminist theory and in the arts: how to produce and to in-
sist on the cultural and libidinal space for women's bodies
to take their place in a universal up to now dominated by
men; how to produce new spaces as/for women; how to
make knowledges and technologies work for women rather
than simply reproduce themselves according to men's representations of women.

In consideration of architecture, cities, and the future, I want to present a series of very brief postulates, or working hypotheses, to help think the connection between them: postulates that bear less on architecture than perhaps they do on the notion of futurity and the new. I do not want to engage particularly in predicting or making projections onto possible futures, but rather to explore how the very concept of the new and futurity (at least as they are presently embodied) impact on and may help reconfigure the way that bodies, cities, and their relations are thought.

1. Fantasies about the future are always, at least in part, projections, images, hopes, and horrors extrapolated from the present, though not simply from the present situation but from its cultural imaginary, its self-representation, its own latencies or virtualities. Whether self-fulfilling and thus prophetic, or wildly fictionalized, these fantasies represent neuralgic points of present investment and anxiety, loci of intense vulnerability, anxiety, or optimism. In this sense, they are more revealing of the status and permeability of the present than they are indices of transformation or guarantees of a present-to-be.

2. Cities have always represented and projected images and fantasies of bodies, whether individual, collective, or political. In this sense, the city can be seen as a (collective) body-prosthesis or boundary that enframes, protects, and houses while at the same time taking its own forms and functions from the (imaginary) bodies it constitutes. Simultaneously, cities are loci that produce, regulate, and structure bodies. This relation is not a simple one of mu-

tual determination nor a singular, abstract diagram of interaction: it depends on the types of bodies (racial, ethnic, class, sexual) and the types of cities (economic, geographic, political), and it is immensely complicated through various relations of intrication, specification, interpolation, and inscription that produce "identities" for both cities in their particularity and populations in their heterogeneity. This relation is not one of "multiple determinations," with the axes of class, race, and sex all systematically interlocked on the one plane, while the types of city—industrialized, commercial, based on one or several industries, a port, located in urban or rural spaces—can be mapped on one another. Rather, it is a relation of both productive constraint and inherent unpredictability: neither relation is able to take place on the one plane or in a regulated form. While the relations between bodies and cities are highly complex and thoroughly saturated with behavioral, regulative, psychical, legal, and communitarian components, nonetheless the corporeality of cities and the materiality of bodies—the relations of exchange and production, habit, conformity, breakdown, and upheaval—have yet to be adequately thought as corporeal. The corporeality, or materiality, of the city is of the same order of complexity as that of bodies. What that corporeality might consist of, what counts as corporeal or material, is not so readily decidable, but it is clear that unless language, representations, structures, patterns, and habits are considered constitutive ingredients of corporeality, then the complexities of neither bodies nor cities are capable of being understood.

3. In the West, bodies and cities in their broad generality—and those discourses aimed at understanding them (cultural studies, urban studies, geography, as well as philosophy, psychology, and feminism)—are (as is always the case) undergoing major structural and pragmatic changes, changes necessitated and brought about by the complex

linkage between global corporatism, the technological revolution in information storage and retrieval, and the transformation of global communications thereby effected. Since the introduction of the personal computer, since the computerization of economic transactions, since the advent of the Internet and instantaneous global communication through cellular phones, satellite networks, and the World Wide Web, transformations in how we understand ourselves, our bodies, our place in cities and communities, and our relation to the future have all been effected, transformations that are in the process of perhaps reconfiguring how we are in the world. Our simultaneous anxiety and joy reside in the extrapolated hopes and fears that an exponentially growing technology promises: its "gift" to us is an increasing edginess about what the future holds in store, whether it promotes our every fantasy to the status of the attainable or the real, or whether we and our hopes are transformed beyond recognition into something other than what we are now.

4. This transformation in technology—let us call it computerization for short—is not simply the creation of a new tool or device more sophisticated than the rest but fundamentally the same in nature. Rather, global computerization is a mode of transformation of the very notion of tool or technology itself. The space, time, logic, and materiality of computerization threaten to disrupt and refigure the very nature of information and communication, as well as the nature of space, time, community, and identity. These technologies make possible knowledges/sciences, modes of art and representation, forms of communication and interaction, that not only are reconfiguring social and personal life but are also, in a fundamental sense, beyond the knowledge and the control of individuals and communities. These technologies, whose limits are unknown by their designers and foremost researchers, have become

subject to historical, perhaps even evolutionary processes or laws that we do not, and perhaps even cannot, know in advance. Computerization transcends the tool or mere cultural innovation, insofar as it has begun an inherently unforeseeable trajectory in global life. Such unforeseen trajectories are not new; they are the forces that shape global transformation, whether dictated by shifts in polar ice caps or the production of nuclear weapons. Technological transformation is not inherently different in its global effect. This is why it may be understood more in the long-term horizon of evolution rather than in the short-term horizon of development or historical change.

5. These technologies have served not to transform bodies in any significant way—at least not yet—but to fundamentally transform the way that bodies are conceived, their sphere of imaginary and lived representation. They promise (and for some they achieve) the fantasy of action, communication, and connectedness at-a-distance, the fantasy of an alternative or virtual existence that may bypass the gravity and weightiness of the body itself: they have mediated spatial relations through the compression of temporal relations, they have transformed interaction and communication through screen and virtual mediation, they have transformed the notion of community through selective global expansion. Bodies clearly are, and always have been, the objects of prosthetic transformation and supplementation, of virtual enhancement and technical mediation. Computerization does not transform this prosthetic hankering; rather, it transforms its degrees of intimacy with the body, the size and nature of prosthetic intervention: micromachines cleaning out veins and arteries, microcomputers pulsating as heart or lung enhancements. It transforms an imaginary anatomy well beyond its technological capacities, yielding the fantasy of the interchangeability, even transcendence, of the body and its corporeal configuration.

6. Yet, while the capacity for technological transformation and supplementation of the body is unforeseeable, it is only as, with, and through the body (the body insofar as it can incorporate technology, not only into its operations and functions but into its imaginary self-conception) that such technology is possible and useful. The supersession and transcendence of the body is impossible. The body's limits—whatever they might be, and it is clear that we have no idea how to even ascertain an answer—are the limits of technological invention. Bodies can incorporate and be modeled by and as technology according to what they can accommodate. Technology is the limit of the body, its most "external" as well as "internalized" reach. Technology in this sense is necessarily tied not to a subject or a community but to bodily capacities and imaginaries.

7. Thus, a final hypothesis: to the degree that technology is in the process of transforming bodies (at times imperceptibly and at other times markedly), only to that degree is it capable of transforming cities. The mode of futurity, that is, of becoming, is a condition of bodily existence (this is what evolution teaches us, if it teaches anything at all): it is also the life and existence of the city. The technological does not threaten to supersede cities as we know them, for their transformation is in resonance with the transformations of the body. The cities of the future will almost certainly resemble cities as we know them today only to the extent that bodies will resemble our own and function according to their various modalities. In this sense, cities of the future, like cities of the present, will not be imposed on an unwilling populace, that is, from outside. The bodies of the populace require spatial conditions, connections between each other, and various locations that both map and interact with the bodies of cities, their modes of operation, their technological accomplishments and requirements.

Part Two *Transitional Spaces*

Thinking is not innate, but must be engendered in thought. . . . The problem is not to direct or methodologically apply a thought which preexists in principle and in nature, but to bring into being that which does not yet exist (there is no other work, *all the rest is arbitrary, mere decoration). To think is to create—there is no other creation.*

Gilles Deleuze, *Difference and Repetition*

Modern thought, from its inception and in its very density, is a certain mode of action. . . . Thought had already "left" itself in its own being as early as the nineteenth century; it is no longer theoretical. As soon as it functions, it offends or reconciles, attracts or repels, breaks, dissociates, unites or reunites; it cannot help but liberate or enslave. . . . At the level of its existence, in its very dawning, [thought] is in itself an action—a perilous act.

Michel Foucault, *The Order of Things*

1. Thinking

A text, whether book, paper, film, painting, or building, can be thought of as a kind of thief in the night. Furtive, clandestine, and always complex, it steals ideas from all around, from its own milieu and history, and better still from its outside, and disseminates them elsewhere. It is not only a conduit for the circulation of ideas, as knowledges or truths, but a passage or point of transition from one (social) stratum or space to another. A text is not the repository of knowledges or truths, the site for the storage of information (and thus in imminent danger of obsolescence from the "revolution" in storage and retrieval that information technology has provided as its provocation to the late twentieth century), so much as it is a process of scattering thought; scrambling terms, concepts, and practices; forging linkages; becoming a form of action. A text is not simply a tool or an instrument; seeing it as such makes it too utilitarian, too amenable to intention, too much designed for a subject. Rather, it is explosive, dangerous, volatile. Like concepts, texts are the products of the intermingling of old and new, a complexity of internal coherences or consistencies and external referents, of intension and extension, of thresholds and becomings. Texts, like concepts, do things, make things, perform connections, bring about new alignments.

Instead of a Derridean model of the text as textile, as interweaving—which produces a closed, striated space of intense overcodings, a fully semiotized model of textuality (a model that is gaining considerable force in architectural and urbanist discourses)—texts could, more in keeping with the thinking of Gilles Deleuze, be read and used more productively as little bombs that, when they do not explode in one's face (as bombs are inclined to do), scatter thoughts and images into different linkages or new alignments without necessarily destroying them. Ideally, they produce unexpected intensities, peculiar sites of indifference, new connections with other objects, and thus generate affective and conceptual transformations that problematize, challenge, and move beyond existing intellectual and pragmatic frameworks. Instead of the eternal status of truth, or the more provisional status of knowledge, texts have highly provisional or short-term effects, though they may continue to be read for generations. They only remain effective and alive, however, if they have effects, if they shake things up, produce realignments. In

Deleuzian terms, such a text, such thought, could be described as fundamentally moving, "nomadological" or "rhizomatic."[1]

How to *think* architecture differently? How to think *in* architecture, or *of* architecture, without conforming to the standard assumptions, the doxa, the apparent naturalness, or rather the evolutionary fit assumed to hold between being and building? How to move beyond the pervasive presumption that subjectivity and dwelling exist in a relation of complementarity, either a relation of containment (space or dwelling contains or houses subjects) or a relation of expression (space or dwelling as the aesthetic or pragmatic expression of subjectivity)? How to see dwelling as something other than the containment or protection of subjects? In short, how to think architecture beyond complementarity and binarization, beyond subjectivity and signification? This is a question that cannot afford easy answers: for ready-made answers become a blockage for thought, for architecture, for building and creating. It is a question that thus cannot and should not be answered but must be continually posed, rigorously raised in such a way as to defy answers, whenever architecture, or for that matter any disciplinary practice, sinks comfortably into routine, into formulas, accepted terms, agreed-upon foundations, an accepted history of antecedents, or a pregiven direction.

Deleuze's project, both in collaboration with Félix Guattari and alone, is in part about thinking, about how to think, to think while making or rather while doing: to think *as* doing. What is the place of philosophy in architecture, or of architecture in philosophy? Could it be that Deleuze's work has something to offer in rethinking architecture? Or conversely, and equally plausibly: Is architecture not antithetical to the Deleuzian endeavor? Can there be such a thing as Deleuzian architecture, perhaps in analogous fashion to the (relatively) easy absorption of the work of Jacques Derrida into architecture through a partially bizarre reading of deconstruction and poststructuralism, terms that have parallel trajectories in architecture and philosophy?[2] Can architecture incorporate/appropriate—that is, cannibalize—nomadology or rhizomatics as readily as it has deconstruction? With what effects might such a meeting, ingestion, or conjunction occur?

Deleuze's work seems to lend itself to a certain understanding of space, spatialization, and movement: his preference for geography over the typical privileging of history by philosophy is well known,[3] as are his metaphorics of territorialization and deterritorialization, and his fascination with baroque art, philosophy, and architecture.[4] At the same time, he seems to disdain the pervasive architectural models that have dominated the history of philosophy—knowledge and its foundations, the edifice of truth, material base and ideological superstructure, even the tree of knowledge—which philosophy has needed in order to develop its own self-conception. If Deleuze is the great nomadologist, the thinker of movement, of difference, the cartographer of force rather than form, if his goal is to produce a certain quaking, or perhaps stuttering,[5] then his work may provide a point of mobilization in the ongoing movement to destabilize and rethink architecture.

To "introduce" Deleuze to architecture is, in any case, a strange proposition. It remains unclear how this could be accomplished, given that the Deleuzian enterprise is so resistant to the notion of "application" (theory is not so much to be applied as to be used). When Deleuzian concepts are transported to other areas, jargon-filled replications of the terminology are spawned, but not the disordering effects of the analysis.[6] Of course, Deleuze's work is not beyond appropriation or application—on the contrary, not only have his writings been happily incorporated into the visual arts[7] but his concepts have been wrenched out of context and applied willy-nilly to all manner of objects and relations.[8] I am concerned here less with "applying" Deleuzian concepts to the architectural field than with raising some questions inspired by the Deleuzian project of reconceiving thought in order to avoid coming up with recuperable answers, in order to unsettle or make architecture itself, if not stutter, then tremble. Consequently, there is no single Deleuzian text, nor any specific architectural program, that I want to explore here: instead, I would like to examine how Deleuze's reconceptualization of thought itself may have ramifying effects for architecture.

For Deleuze, philosophy is a site for the invention of concepts. Concepts can no longer be understood as self-contained nuggets of mental contents, nor as the blurred product of continuous streams of consciousness, but are complex assemblages perhaps best understood in terms of *hecceities*, as event or advent. Thought results from the provocation of an encounter. Thought is what confronts us from the outside, unexpectedly: "Something in the world forces us to think."[9] Thought confronts us necessarily from the outside, from outside the concepts we already have, from outside the subjectivities we already are, from outside the material reality we already know.[10] Thinking involves a wrenching of concepts away from their usual configurations, outside the systems in which they have a home, and outside the structures of recognition that constrain thought to the already known.[11] Thinking is never easy. Thought-events, like language-bodies, are singularities, which mix with and have effects on other materialities, with political, cultural, cinematic, or architectural events. Deleuze is the great theorist of difference, of thought as difference.

Derrida's work has had a surprisingly powerful effect on the discourses of architecture and urban planning—surprising because his interests *seem* so philosophical, so textually based and hermetically self-contained. The central Derridean notion of *différance*, or the trace, entails a notion of constitutive inscription: before the word and the thing, before the distinction between space and its "contents," texts and their "ideas," is an originary and impossible trace or difference that always infects the purity of the container with the impurity of its contents, and vice versa. Up to now, Derrida seems to have signaled the limit of tolerance of the "sciences of space" to "postmodern" (that is, French) philosophy. It remains to be seen whether Deleuze will be so happily accommodated.

Unlike Derrida who conceives of thought, or representation, as *différance*—that is, as deferral and detour, as the failure to reach a destination, instead of seeing difference as the inherent impossibility of presence (a project that is not without its effects in shaking up the singularity and self-sameness of the Logos)—Deleuze thinks difference primarily as force, as *affirmation*, as action, as precisely effectivity. Thought is active force, positive desire, which *makes* a difference, whether in the image form in the visual and cinematic arts, in the built form in architecture, or in concept form in philosophy. Deleuze's project thus involves the reenergization of thought, the affirmation of life and change, and an attempt to work around those forces of antiproduction that aim to restrict innovation and prevent change: to free lines, points, concepts, events, from the structures and constraints that bind them to the same, to the one, to the self-identical.[12]

Deleuze's project then is to free thought from that which captures or captivates it, to free thought from the image, indeed to free thought from representation, from the "transcendental illusions of representation," to give it back its capacity to effect transformation or metamorphosis, to make thinking itself a little bomb or scattergun:

Thought is primarily trespass and violence, the enemy, and nothing presupposes philosophy: everything begins with misosophy. Do not count upon thought to ensure the relative necessity of what it thinks. Rather, count upon the contingency of an encounter with that which forces thought to raise up and educate the absolute necessity of an act of thought or a passion to think. The conditions of a true critique and a true creation are the same: the destruction of an image of thought which presupposes itself and the genesis of the act of thinking in thought itself.[13]

The four illusions of representation[14] veil the genesis and functioning of thought, for they separate a force from what it can do, and thus function as modes of reaction, as the conversion of active force into reactive force, in the terminology of Deleuze's *Nietzsche and Philosophy*. This veiling of the thought is identified with a refusal of difference. Through these various tactics, pervasive in the history of Western philosophy, thought loses its force of difference, its positive productivity, and is subordinated to sameness, becomes reactive. If the goal of the intellectual is not simply the production of knowledge but, more precisely, the production of concepts, of thought, and if the disciplines, including architecture and philosophy, function to thwart thought, to stifle and prevent exploration, to inhibit the production of the new, then the function of the radical intellectual, whether philosopher or architect, is to struggle against whatever, in discourse and in practice, functions to prevent thought—which for Deleuze are the regimes of subjectification, signification, and representation that continually bind thought to unity or the

One. It is as if the forces of knowledge and power cannot tolerate difference—the new, the unthought, the outside—and do all they can to suppress it, by forcing it to conform to expectation, to fit into a structure, to be absorbable, assimilable, and digestible without disturbance or perturbation.

The question remains: How to disturb architecture, given the tendency of some architectural theorists to take in whatever seems outrageous without it seeming to have any effect or make any difference? How to infect architecture with its outside? In other words, how to force an encounter, to effect a transformation or becoming, in which the series that is architecture can be intercut with an element (or several) from its outside, from that series which is philosophy, in which the two series are thereby transformed through their encounter: the becoming-philosophy of architecture can only be effected through the becoming-architecture of philosophy. Deleuze poses a new understanding of difference, in which thought (thought in concepts, thought in images, thought in building materials) asserts its full force as event, as material modification, as movement beyond. Insofar as architecture is seeking not so much "innovation," not simply "the latest fad," but to produce differently, to engender the new, to risk creating otherwise, Deleuze's work may be of some help, although it remains unclear more precisely how. This unclarity is not the risk Deleuze's work poses, but its wager or problem (for thought is provoked by problems): How to keep architecture open to its outside, how to force architecture to *think*?

2. The Outside

In a certain sense, all of Deleuze's works, as Deleuze makes clear in his reading of Foucault, are about the outside, the unthought, the exterior, the surface, the simulacrum, the fold, lines of flight, what resists assimilation, what remains foreign even within a presumed identity, whether this is the intrusion of a minor language into a majoritarian one or the pack submerged within an individual. The outside or exterior is what both enables and resists the movements of territorialization and deterritorialization. It is what resists the globalizing sweep of the by now well-worn postmodern catchphrase "there is no outside" (of discourse, of patriarchy, of history, of power), a formula that encapsulates the lures of signification and subjectification. What plays the role of the excluded or expelled in Derrida's work functions in terms of the outside in Deleuze.

Can the effects of depth, of interiority, of domesticity and privacy be generated by the billowing convolutions and contortions of an outside, a skin? What does the notion of outside, exterior, or surface do that displaces the privilege of interiority, architecturally, philosophically, and subjectively? The boundary between the inside and the outside, just as much as between self and other and subject and object, must not be regarded as a limit to be transgressed, so much as a boundary to be traversed. As Brian Massumi stresses in *The Politics of Everyday Fear*, boundaries are only produced in the process of passage: boundaries do not so much define the routes of passage; it is movement that defines and constitutes boundaries. These boundaries, consequently, are more porous and less fixed and rigid than is commonly understood, for there is already an infection by one side of the border of the other; there is a becoming otherwise of each of the terms thus bounded.

It is significant that Deleuze, like Derrida, does not attempt to abandon binarized thought or to replace it with an alternative; rather, binarized categories are played off each other, are rendered molecular, global, and are analyzed in their molar particularities, so that the possibilities of their reconnections, their realignment in different "systems," are established. So it is not as if the outside or the exterior must remain eternally counterposed to an interiority that it contains: rather, the outside is the transmutability of the inside. Presumably for this reason Deleuze wants to link the outside not with the inside but with the *real*. This is in no way to align the inside with the unreal, the possible, or the imaginary; it is to see that the outside is a *virtual* condition of the inside, as equally real,[15] as time is the virtual of space. The virtual is immanent in the real.

Thought is a confrontation or encounter with an outside. Deleuze deals with this notion of the outside primarily in two texts, *Foucault* and *Cinema 2: The Time-Image*. Following a tradition perhaps initiated by Nietzsche, and following a zigzagging path through Artaud to Blanchot,[16] Deleuze sees in Foucault, as we ourselves may see in Deleuze, the culmination of this confrontation between thought and its outside, between thought and the unthought. This conception of the outside or the unthought is already developed in Foucault's archaeological period, most notably in *The Order of Things*, where Foucault suggests that man and the unthought are born simultaneously, as twin products of the nineteenth century: where Descartes had brought together consciousness and thought, modern thought dates from the rise of both man and the unthought:

Man and the unthought are, at the archaeological level, contemporaries. Man has not been able to describe himself as a configuration in the *episteme* without thought at the same time discovering, both in itself and outside itself, at its borders yet also in its very warp and woof, an element of darkness, an apparently inert density in which it is embedded, an unthought (whatever name we give it) is not lodged in man like a shriveled-up nature or stratified history; it is in relation to man, the Other.[17]

In the final chapter of *Foucault*, Deleuze develops this idea of the necessity of an outside and shows that it remains an ongoing concern in Foucault's writings, from his archaeological period through to his final writings. Deleuze suggests that in Foucault's final, ethical works there is no abandonment of his commitment either to the materiality of his various objects of analysis or to the peculiarly "outside," or estranged, pragmatic reading of subjectivity or textuality that Foucault posed, no return to anything like a phenomenological or psychological framework. These last works continue, but perhaps inflect, the trajectory of the outside already well-formulated in Foucault's earlier texts. Deleuze relates this trajectory to the question of interiority: Does Foucault present an analysis of interiority? What sort of interior might this be? Does Foucault's orientation to the issue of ethical self-formation mean that he is now committed to a notion of (subjective or psychical) interiority?

Up to now [in Foucault's work] we have encountered three dimensions: the relations which have been formed or formalized along certain strata (Knowledge); the relations between forces to be found at the level of the diagram (Power); and the relation with the outside, that absolute relation with the outside . . . which is also a non-relation (Thought). Does this mean there is no inside? Foucault continually submits interiority to a radical critique. . . . The outside is not a fixed limit but moving matter animated by peristaltic movements, folds and foldings that altogether make up an inside: they are not something other than the outside, but precisely the inside of an outside.[18]

Deleuze here describes three characteristics of a relation between two series (which he describes in terms of statements and visibilities in *Foucault*, but in very different terms in other texts). First, the relations can be understood only insofar as each series is separate from the other, creating its own "zones of proximity," its own modes of functioning. Second, insofar as both series are located in an outside, this outside is capable of asserting itself on the inside, the series it produces (statements, visibilities): these function as the unsaid or the unseen within discourse or representation. Third, insofar as both series are modified through the encounter of each with the other, with the drawing of lines to link them, they are capable of interactions or becomings. More than a *description* of Foucault's claim, this is a general or abstract articulation of Deleuze's own position (which is no doubt true of all of Deleuze's writings: they are as much a reflection of his "methodology" as they are rigorous and attuned readings of texts marginalized in the history of philosophy). For Deleuze's Foucault, the inside is an effect of the outside: the inside is a fold or doubling of the outside, a contortion of the exterior surface: "It resembles exactly the invagination of a tissue in embryology, or the act of doubling in sewing: twist, fold, stop and so on."[19]

In Deleuze's understanding of the time-image in cinema, the outside is what displaces the inside, what burrows from without to effect an interiority. The problem is posed to concepts, to thinking, from/as the outside, an outside that can only appear to thought as the unthought, and to sight as the unseen. The outside insinuates itself into thought, drawing knowledge outside of itself, outside of what is expected, producing a hollow which it can then inhabit—an outside within or as the inside:

Far from restoring knowledge, or the internal certainty that it lacks, to thought, the problematic deduction puts the unthought into thought, because it takes away all its interiority to excavate an outside in it, an irreducible reverse-side, which consumes its substance. Thought finds itself taken over by the exteriority of a "belief," outside any interiority of a "belief," outside any interiority of a mode of knowledge.[20]

This outside cannot be equated with Kantian noumena, with a prelinguistic Real (as in Lacanian psychoanalysis), or with an independent confirmable world (as empiricists claim). What is truly radical in Deleuze's understanding is his claim that this outside must be thought itself[21] or perhaps even life itself.[22] The series are themselves the folds of an outside, constituted out of the same stuff. Thought is projected, captured, pinned down, insofar as it is caught up in the networks of power, knowledge, and subjectification:

The question: "What does thinking signify? What do we call thinking?" is the arrow first fired by Heidegger and then again by Foucault. He writes a history, but a history of thought as such. To think means to experiment and to problematize. Knowledge, power and self are the triple root of a problematization of thought. In the field of knowledge as problem thinking is first of all seeing and speaking, but thinking is carried out in the space between the two, in the interstice or disjunction between seeing and speaking.[23]

It is not in the convergence but in the disjunction of series that the outside is active in the production of an inside. This may be why, for Deleuze, the middle is always the privileged point to begin, why thought is perhaps best captured *in between*. Thought starts in the middle, at the point of intersection of two series, events, or processes which, however temporarily, share a common milieu. The interiority of these series is of less interest than the way these two series are capable of being aligned to connect, to create their plane of consistence or coexistence, which is made possible through the operations of this outside. Becoming is the way in which each of the two series can transform: becoming is bodily thought,[24] the ways in which thought, force, or change, invests and invents new series, metamorphosing new bodies from the old through their encounter.[25] Becoming is what enables a trait, a line, an orientation, an event to be released from the system, series, organism, or object that may have the effect of transforming the whole, making it no longer function singularly: it is an encounter between bodies that releases something from each and, in the process, releases or makes real a virtuality, a series of enabling and transforming possibilities. Becoming-animal only makes sense insofar as *both* the subject and the animal are transformed in the encounter.[26]

Thought is what comes between a cause and its habitual effect, between one being and another, a fissure between strata that allows something from them to escape, to ramify. It is an unhinging—perhaps a deranging—of expectation, order, organization, to replace them not with disorder or disorganization but with reordering. Rather than assuming a pure positivity, the jamming effects of thought do not simply actively produce (new thoughts and new things or assemblages) but intervene, to insert a stammer, a hesitation or pause within the expected; thought may actively function to passively interrupt habit and expectation by allowing something already there in the series, in the subject or object, to become.[27] Thought, life, is that space outside the actual which is filled with virtualities, movements, trajectories that need release. It is what a body is capable of doing without necessity and without being captured by what it habitually does, a sea of (possible) desires and machines waiting their chance, their moment of actualization.

3. Building

This notion of the outside may prove to be of some relevance to architecture. Indeed, it is doubly relevant, for it signals the notion of an outside as the edifice or exterior of a building, as well as a broader notion of the outside of architectural discipline itself—a spatial as well as a nonspatial outside. Can architecture, like both subjectivity and signification—two models that have dominated the contemporary forms of its theoretical self-reflections—be rethought in terms of the outside, in terms of surfaces, in terms of a certain flatness, in terms of dynamism and movement rather than stasis or the sedentary? Can architecture inhabit us as much as we see ourselves inhabiting it? Does architecture have to be seen in terms of subjectivization and semiotization, in terms of use and meaning? Can architecture be thought, no longer as a whole, a complex unity, but as a set of and site for becomings of all kinds? What would such an understanding entail?

In short, can architecture be thought, in connection with other series, as assemblage? What would this entail? What are the implications of opening up architectural discourses to Deleuzian desire-as-production? Can architecture work (its or an) *outside*? What is it to open up architecture to thought, to force, to life, to the outside? By outside I do not mean the practical, financial, and aesthetic exigencies of building design and construction, nor even the demands on architecture to align with the environment, a landscape, interior design, interior or exterior artworks, which in a certain sense are all "inside" architecture and its history, part of the necessary structure of compromise that produces a building as a commodity. Rather, I refer here to what is alien, other, different from or beyond it. Can architecture survive such assaults on its autonomy? Can it become something—many things—other than what it is and how it presently functions? If its present function is an effect of the crystallization of its history within, inside, its present, can its future be something else?

These are also questions that Derrida has helped architecture pose to itself—the question of the indeterminacy of address, the openness of all systems to the undoings the future proposes—but they are formulated, albeit in different terms and with different aims and effects, through Deleuze's writings as well. Deleuze may be seen to share certain of Derrida's political concerns;[28] nonetheless, his work offers something quite different from Derrida's architectural contributions and appropriations. Deleuze remains a philosopher throughout: when he analyzes artworks, when he explores architecture, when he interrogates cinema or literature, it is in terms of their concepts, their modes of thinking-doing, their movements, crossovers, and linkages with philosophical issues, systems, and texts that he draws out or diagrams. This is not to say that he subordinates them to philosophy, makes them simply philosophical illustrations, or the objects or occasions of philosophical speculation. Rather, he is interested in the autonomy, the specificity of these different practices and their modes or manner of interchange with their outside. These are the two series he interrogates together—art, literature, cinema, science or architecture, and philosophy—seeking their plane of consistency and their modes of becoming.

Where Derrida could be described as the philosopher who insists on bringing the outside, the expelled, repressed, or excluded, into the inside by showing the constitutive trace it must leave on that which must expel it (that is, the impossibility of keeping borders and delimitations clear-cut), Deleuze could be understood as the philosopher who evacuates the inside (whether of a subject, an organism, or a text), forcing it to confront its outside, evacuating it and thereby unloosing its systematicity or organization, its usual or habitual functioning, allowing a part, function, or feature to spin off or mutate into a new organization or system, to endlessly deflect, become, make. If we are no longer to explore the textuality of building—its immersion in discourses, its textual implications and investments, its own modes of marking, as Derrideanism entails—but to explore the possibilities of becoming, the virtualities latent in building, the capacity of buildings to link with and make other series deflect and transform while being transformed in the process, Deleuze's work may prove crucial. I am not able to address this possibility adequately in specifically architectural terms; it is something for those trained or working in architecture: the question of the unthought, the unbuilt, the outside *for architecture* itself. It is a question that I believe needs to be posed in all seriousness whenever the formulaic and the predictable take over from experimentation and innovation, realignment and transformation.

An awful lot of hype surrounds not only computer technologies but also their collective product, the Net, and the Net's most fantasy-laden component, cyberspace. Much of this commotion is due to a fascination with what the digital telecommunications revolution and its associated soft- and hardwares promise but have yet to deliver. In their nascent incompleteness, indeed in a form still more dreamlike than actual, these technologies are ripe, as it were, for various imaginary schemas, projected futures, dreams, hopes, and fears. Just as the emergence of steam, electrical, telephonic, and other technologies clearly exerted powerful effects on the imaginations of the populaces in which they appeared (which seem to decrease to the degree that these technologies become normalized and socially integrated into the banalities of everyday life), exponential growth has also occurred not simply in technological advances but more significantly in cultural fantasies surrounding the eruption of new and altogether different futures from those we had previously envisaged. Cyberspace and virtual reality (VR) represent arguably the most intensely concentrated focal points for this phantasmatic explosion, firing the imaginations not only of the technologically literate but of those interested in entertainment, knowledge, and information—in short, of global populations.

Digital technologies have transformed the storage, circulation, and retrieval of information by transforming information of all kinds into binary form and reducing

Five **Cyberspace, Virtuality, and the Real: Some Architectural Reflections**

matter into silicon and liquid-crystal traces (the chip and the screen). Perhaps the most striking transformation effected by these technologies is the change in our perceptions of materiality, space, and information, which is bound directly or indirectly to affect how we understand architecture, habitation, and the built environment. These changes are most apparent in the development of complex systems of simulation, storage, and circulation of information and representation now labeled cyberspace and virtual reality. Cyberspace has been considered a "parallel" universe to our own, generated and sustained by global communications networks and computers linking disparate physical spaces and individuals through a shared virtual space, the space of linked, networked computers and their users.[1] The contours of this virtual space and its various contents can be generated, manipulated, and to some extent controlled in ways unheard of in the space(s) that we normally take for granted, which I will describe as lived, everyday space.

The simultaneous fascination and horror evoked by such technologies may result from how they are seen to supplant or replace those technologies to which we are accustomed, which we now designate as "real" and which we no longer see as technological interventions but as modes of everyday operation in the real. (An initial hypothesis: the virtual is not a pure, self-sufficient realm with its own fixed features and characteristics. Rather, it is a relative or differential concept whose status as virtual requires an actual relative to which its virtuality can be marked as such.)

The simulated environments offered by the Net and VR technologies have generated heated debate between two equally stringent and, I believe, equally naive, groups. On the one hand are the technophiles and cybernauts who see in this technology the key to new spaces, new identities, and new relations, in short, new worlds, open and available, tailored to one's individual predilections and tastes—that is, who see in VR the potential for a world of unfettered choice. They believe there will be a choice not only of spaces, sites, and environments but also of bodies, subjectivities, and modes of interactions with others: "Cyberspace will not merely provide new experiences . . . it will change what humans perceive themselves to be, at a very fundamental and personal level. In cyberspace, there is no need to move about in a body like the one you possess in physical reality."[2]

Whereas many see in VR the ability to aspire to God-like status, to create, live in, and control worlds, to have a power of simulation that surpasses or bypasses the uncontrollable messiness of the real, others (sometimes even the same writers) revile and fear VR's transformation of relations of sociality and community, physicality and corporeality, location and emplacement, sexuality, personal intimacy, and shared work space—the loss of immediacy, of physical presence. These individuals may lament the replacement of face-to-face contact with connections established only through electronic mediation or the transformation and reduction of sexual relations from the directness of the bed to the immense technical mediations required for synchronous or asynchronous teledildonics.

Unashamed apologists of cybertechnologies and nostalgic Luddites yearning for days gone by see VR as a powerful force of liberation and a form of ever-encroaching fascistic control, respectively. In a sense these technologies carry both possibilities; but rather than explore technological potential and its relevance to architectural practice—something I am unfortunately unable to do—I hope to see, more broadly and philosophically, how conceptions of virtuality, simulation, computer reproduction and rendering transform our understanding of the real, matter, space, the body, and the world. Neither idealizing nor reviling these emerging technologies, I hope to explore potentialities that are not clearly or simply associated with cybertechnologies alone but are latent in the very idea of futurity.

I must confess that I don't know much about computers. But I know that I like them. I like them not simply because they are incredibly convenient labor-saving tools or devices (I would like my vacuum cleaner if the same were true of it, though in fact we have merely a passing familiarity) but because the computer and the worlds it generates reveal that the world in which we live, the real world, has always been a space of virtuality. The real is saturated with the spaces of projection, possibility, and the new that we now designate as virtual in order to keep them contained behind the glassy smoothness of the computer screen. My computer makes this clear to me, although if I had thought more carefully about the strangeness of writing, of inscription, I would have seen the virtual there too, just as rich and rife with potential as cyberspace itself. The virtual reality of computer space is fundamentally no different from the virtual reality of writing, reading, drawing, or even thinking: the virtual is the space of emergence of the new, the unthought, the unrealized, which at every moment loads the presence of the present with supplementarity, redoubling a world through parallel universes, universes that might have been. I want to explore what the passion for the computer and the attachment to its virtual images, spaces, and projects entails for the notions of habitation that govern architecture, urban design, and the psychologies of inhabitation.

The concept of virtuality has been with us a remarkably long time. It is a coherent and functional idea already in Plato's writings, where both ideas and simulacra exist in some state of virtuality. Instead of too closely identifying it with the invention of new technologies—as is the current obsession—we must realize that since there has been writing (in the Derridean sense of trace—that is, *as the very precondition* of culture itself), there has been some idea of the virtual. The text we read may be in real space, but to the extent that it is comprehensible to us, it also exists in a state of virtuality. We did not have to wait for the computer screen or the movie projector in order to enter virtual space; we have been living in its shadow more or less continually.

Yet significantly, and in spite of much of the accompanying rhetoric, the capacity for simulation clearly has sensory and corporeal limits that are rarely acknowledged, especially because the technology is commonly characterized as a mode of decorporealization and dematerialization. While the computer and its modes of simulation work with remarkable ease and offer pleasure in the visual realm, where we can enjoy the sight of virtual objects in virtual spaces, it is less clear whether we can draw a distinction between the virtual and the real in other perceptual modalities: it is hard to see what would constitute virtual sound and how it could be distinguished from "real" sound.[3] Moreover, neither vision nor sound is virtual but rather the *objects* and *spaces* that vision and sound find as their fields of play. Vision, sound, touch, taste, and smell function in their same modalities as always. VR works, if and when it does, only on the assumption that the senses function as they always have, even in the face of perceptual inputs that have been drastically altered. Virtual objects are now capable of generating the same perceptual effects as "real" objects.

Jacques Lacan, in his earliest writings, ponders the intriguing attraction that specular images exert for the subject in the process of formation. When a real object is reflected in a mirror image, the mirror contains behind its surface an object in a relation of inverted identity with the real object, existing in virtual space, the space behind the plane of the mirror. The mirror surface creates a virtual field that reflects the real, duplicating its spatiality and the object's visual characteristics. Gilles Deleuze later identifies a reciprocal interaction between the virtual and the real, an undecidable reversibility, as if the image could take the place of an object and force the object behind the constraints of the mirror's plane. Each makes a certain imperceptible contribution to the other, not adding any particular feature or quality but a depth of potential, a richer resonance. Lacan specifies that only through an encounter with a virtual counterpart, the double, do we acquire an identity; moreover, this identity remains irresolvably split because of an incapacity to resolve the differences between the real and the virtual body and because, in a certain sense, the real contains the space of the virtual image to the degree that the symbolic overcomes or supersedes the specular. In short, Lacan both affirms and undermines the reliance of the real on the space of virtuality, showing the necessity and impossibility of their separation.[4] In a strange and rare congruence if not agreement with Lacan, Deleuze too, in his writings on Henri Bergson and the time-image, affirms that the real is only functional as such, exists in time, through its immersion in virtuality and saturation as the space of virtuality.[5]

The very term *virtual reality* attests to a phantasmatic extension, a bizarre contortion to save not the real (which is inevitably denigrated and condemned) but rather the will, desire, mind, beyond body or matter: this is a real not quite real, not an "actual real," a "really real" but a real whose reality is at best virtual. An equivocation in and of the real. An apparent rather than an actual "real." The two terms strain at each other, wrenching, as I will argue, the reality of the real away from it, converting how we understand the terms thus oxymoronically linked. The real is not so much divested of its status as reality as converted into a different order in which mind/will/desire are the ruling terms and whose matter, whose "real," is stripped away. The transformation of the real through the concept of the virtual interests me here as much as the technologies through which this change in conceptualization is made necessary.

To accomplish this transformation, it may be useful to contest a common misconception of the relation between the virtual and the real. As an example, I quote from a letter describing the conference session on "The Virtual Body" for which I wrote an earlier version of this paper: "Now, with the growing number of Internet communities, the real city is being challenged by the virtual city of the World Wide Web. In the historic city, a body is necessary to sustain oneself; in the new city of the Internet, only a mind need function. What are the implications of this reconfiguration of the mind/body relationship to the continued viability of the city? How will the new collective of cyberspace, one that is conceptual rather than physical, understand the physical body and physical city?"

Explicitly spelled out here is a common set of representations of the (impossible) separation of body from mind, and thus real from virtual, a separation that I want to question, if only to show that the very real effects of virtuality and the virtual dimensions of reality cannot be so readily separated. This relation between the virtual and the real prefigures and is entwined with a whole series of other oppositional terms—among them, mind and body, culture and nature, origin and copy. Just as the separation of body from mind has long been the regulating fantasy not only of the philosophical enterprise but of those practices (including architecture) based on the privilege of its terms (reason, order, truth, light, vision, etc.), so too the relation between the virtual and the real, while generated from a history of philosophy, has ramifications everywhere, from the most global of public spaces (today, the global space of broadcasting) to the most intimate of personal spaces (the space of individual inhabitation, production, and pleasure). It is the task of architecture, among other things, to negotiate how these spaces are to exist in contiguity with each other and how we are to inhabit them in times to come.

Implicit in the quotation above are a series of regulating assumptions that serve as mechanisms of containment regarding the impact of the virtual on the real. Among the most striking assumptions are (1) the separation of VR from the real and the material, the simulation from the original (seeing one as the dematerialization rather than the retranscription of the other); (2) the alignment of the real, historical city with the body and the virtual city of cyberspace with pure mind divested of bodily traces; (3) the linking of the "real" or "historical" city (the cities of the past) with the virtual or future city such that the latter is seen as the technological development, refinement, and replacement of the former (its evolutionary heir); and (4) the belief that the technological development of virtual communities and networks surpasses, displaces, and problematizes the body and, with it, identity and community as we currently know them.

These assumptions are quite typical of the discourses surrounding VR and cyberspace, which tend to be represented as spaces of disembodiment and thus as a new kind of space unconstrained by the limits of corporeality, available for the free exploration of either reason or imagination, or more positively as a space of bodily augmentation and displacement. What seems so alluring about the half-formed promise of VR technologies is the ideal of a world of one's own that one can share with others through consensus but that one can enter or leave at will, over whose movements and processes one can exert a measure of control, and that brings with it a certain guarantee of pleasure without danger. In a sense, these assumptions are not all that far from the conditions necessary to produce the discipline and practice of architecture itself! (A second hypothesis: perhaps all technologies are modeled on architecture and thus implicated in architecture, at least an architecture that conceives of itself as the housing/clothing of bodies, matter, and spaces.)[6]

The ideal of transcending the body, suppressing corporeality, abandoning the sticky mess of material that constitutes our entwinement with the real, seems to have been pervasive throughout both philosophical theory (and through it, architectural discourses) and the mathematical and computational sciences that came together with engineering to design and produce computers and the virtual spaces upon which they now both rely. These disciplines are threaded together through the fantasy of a certain (always only partial) divestment from bodily existence and experience, indeed through a kind of resistance to death itself, here seen as the final limit of a body.

This pervasive fantasy of disembodiment is linked to the fantasy of mastery at a distance, of "tele-presence," the illusion of being able to leave the body at will and reappear elsewhere, to be present while not really present (a fantasy that is powerful in religious obsessions and in New Age belief systems). This fantasy is specifically articulated as such, without the slightest self-consciousness, in the writings of some pioneer figures in the area, and by many of the biggest names working on cyberculture, from Donna Haraway to Howard Rheingold, Michael Benedikt, Allucquère Stone, and William Mitchell. All in one way or another seek, desire, hope, or imagine some kind of liberation, movement beyond and outside the body and its perceptual, sexual, or material limits in the mode of action-at-a-distance (which, significantly and rather strangely, Nietzsche has attributed to women as their special power of allure).

Benedikt clearly articulates this profound somatophobia: "Cyberspace . . . is nothing more or less, than the latest stage in the evolution of [Karl Popper's] *World 3* [the world of social objects, artifacts], *with the ballast of materiality cast away*—cast away again, and perhaps finally."[7] Countless other examples, with more or less sophistication and consistency, can be cited. In a paper that openly acknowledges the ways in which prevailing conceptions of cyberspace are bound up in Cartesian dualism, Marcos Novak nonetheless, within the space of a paragraph, both affirms the inherent corporeality of all spaces, cyberspace notwithstanding, and declares: "If cyberspace holds an immense fascination, it is not simply the fascination of the new. Cyberspace stands to thought as flight stands to crawling."[8] In short, cyberspace is a mode of transcendence, the next quantum leap in the development of mind, as flying transcends the bodily activity of walking. The relation between virtual or cyberspace and real space is conceived throughout as a relation of mind to body, or transcendence to immanence, with all of the hierarchical privileges accorded to the mind in Western thought.

More than most cultural theorists, Allucquère Stone—perhaps because of her dual intellectual investments as emblematic transsexual and as eminent cybertheorist/performer—finds the allure of cyberspace precisely that of transsexualism: the capacity of a supervening subject or mind to choose its body and modes of materiality, claiming experience of multiple subject positions even while appearing to acknowledge the inherent belonging together of any mind in and as a body. While she acknowledges corporeal embeddedness, she is fascinated by the options available to a consciousness that can choose a male or female body, a black or white one: "How do people without bodies make love?"[9] Are there people without bodies? What could they be? If they can transcribe, metamorphose themselves from one corporeal context to another, in what way is a person then embodied? (The very language of embodiment implies a "putting into the body": could this be a residual language of philosophies of disembodiment?) What would making love be without a body? To be fair to Stone, in a number of contexts, her work does quite precisely characterize the status of cyberculture; she does describe cyberspace as a locus of intense desire for refigured embodiment, and thus as something less than the transfiguration of human matter into cybernetic information.

Less self-promoting and ubiquitous theorists, even in their more self-aware moments, seem stuck within the conundrum: to supersede a Cartesian division between mind and body through notions of cyberspace is surreptitiously to reintroduce it where it seems most readily vanquished: "A grand paradox is in operation here: even as we are finally abandoning the Cartesian notion of a division of mind and body, we are embarking on an adventure of creating a world that is the precise embodiment of that division. For, it is quite clear that our reality outside cyberspace is the metaphysical plane of cyberspace, that to the body in cyberspace we are the mind, the preexisting soul."[10]

I am less concerned about this separation of mind from body, and of virtual from physical or real—although how it is possible to escape the body and the real is unclear to me, even or especially as one dons one's virtual gloves and goggles or lights up that necessary cigarette and prepares coffee to begin a heavy session on the computer—

than I am about how cyberspace and the space of virtuality require us to rethink matter and corporeality to accommodate their strange meanderings. I am less interested in the displacement from the physical to the conceptual, from the body to the mind, because I do not believe that such a displacement occurs now, or ever. If we don't just have bodies but are bodies (as I have argued elsewhere),[11] there can never be the threat of displacing body in favor of mind or abandoning the real for the virtual. Rather, cyberspace, virtual worlds, and the order of computer simulation—whether imagistic or computational—show that our notions of real, of body, and of the physical or historical city need to be complicated and rethought to accommodate what they seem to oppose. My goal here is to rethink some of the more traditional concepts—the physical, the corporeal, the real, the material—in light of the unhinging that concepts like the virtual and the conceptual propose. These terms continue to refuse their external status as oppositional terms and instead are seen to inhabit the very heart of the real and the material. This virtual is not a geometric, spatial, or technological concept, nor is it structured by phantasmatic or imaginary projections alone; rather, it is the domain of latency or potentiality, given that the boundaries between the virtual and the real or the physical are unsustainable.

What does the concept of cyberspace offer architecture? At least two things: the idea of a disembodied, nonmaterial, or transcendental notion of design, design disembodied from matter; and the idea of a simulation, reproduction, enhancement, or augmentation of the senses and materiality. What role do computers play in architecture? They function primarily as sites of simulation and calculation, as networks of information and exchange.

Is there something distinctive about the computer's architectural inflections? Does computer technology imply a particular modality of the visual simulation of lived or mobile space (the space of cybernetic planning and design), which remains in principle no different from drawings and plans in their more conventional forms? Is computer technology distinctive because of the mobilization, the animation of space that it brings, the simulation of its inhabitation? Is it the capacity for multiple calculations (structural, financial, mathematical, logistic)? These particular modalities and usages seem to preserve intact the fundamental structures of design, marketing, client refinement, and interaction with the profession, speeding up the time of communication while visually enhancing the experience of design. Yet both the space of computer simulation and the reconceptualization of virtuality do threaten to create major upheavals if their consequences and implications are not carefully considered.

More than functioning in the realm of design, planning, and projection, computer technologies are increasingly incorporated into building itself, as one of its devices. Rather than simply being seen as a device or tool at the disposal of the architect, designer, or planner, the latest technology (that is, as an instrument that in no way upsets the purpose for which the instrument or tool is used), the computer threatens, in the words of Roland Barthes, to change the object itself. The virtuality of the space of computing, and of inscription more generally, is transforming at least in part how we understand what it is to be in space (and time). The Net not only speeds up and enhances information storage and retrieval and communications structures, but it threatens to disrupt or reconfigure the very nature of information, communication, and the types of social interaction and movement they require. It threatens to transpose spatial relations into temporal ones (the geographical dislocation of subjects is compensated for on the Net through both the instantaneity of communication and the dislocation of synchronous communications) and community relations into solitary sociality (the Net is mediated through the one-to-one connection between user and computer, even as the user and computer are wired up to the Net).

Can the computer screen act as the clear-cut barrier separating cyberspace from real space, the space of mental inhabitation from the physical space of corporeality? What if the boundary is more permeable than the smooth glassy finality of the screen? What if it is no longer clear where matter converts into information and information is reconfigured as matter or representation? I am thinking here of the implications of the rather wild and newly emergent discipline of artificial life, which has come out of the convergence of biological modeling and mathematical physics and which, like the domain of architectural applications, wants to simulate the (in this case, evolutionary) space of the lived world.

What would be a virtual house? Or is this way of formulating the issue already the problem? This question implies that one can design or build a virtual house within the confines of a real environment, fiddling about with one feature or detail, giving it virtuality in the otherwise bland real without understanding that the entirety of the environment—the real itself—is always already virtual insofar as it is open to time, historicity, and futurity. The relevant question is less "Can one design a virtual house?" than "How can one design in such a way as to bring out the virtualities of building and of the real itself?"

There seem to be two different ways of conceiving of virtuality in architecture: (1) as an entirely new technology developed through the use of computers, a technology that can or should somehow be incorporated into the way that buildings work (security systems, electrical systems, even watering systems are now readily programmable rather than manual tasks); and (2) as an entirely new way of seeing, inhabiting, and designing space. The first concept involves understanding the space of virtuality, cyberspace, as a containable, separable field, entered voluntarily when one enters one's access code into a machine from which one can choose to walk away. (This is how the Net and its associated hardware and software are marketed: as enhancement of existing skills rather than the production of new needs and skills.) The second involves reconceptualizing the real and the relations of embeddedness, the nesting or interimplication (perhaps another name for difference) of the virtual and real within each other.

What does the idea of virtuality, rather than virtual reality, offer to architecture? The idea of an indeterminate, unspecifiable future, open-endedness, the preeminence of futurity over the present and the past, the promise not of simulation (which is a repetition, representation, or re-production of a real or an original—a copy, with its own particular joys and aesthetic delights) but of (temporal) displacement, not simply deferral but endless openness. The idea of open-endedness, indeterminacy of function or telos, or the openness of form needs to be reworked not only in technological terms but more urgently (since technological development seems to have its own often quite different pace) in terms of viable and aesthetic incorporations of an idea of virtuality, of futurity (of retroaction, the continually rewriting, rehabitation, reinvestment of the present so that it is never fully itself). (A third hypothesis: we can only live in the real insofar as it is continually [re]inhabited, reinvested, and reinvented by virtuality.)

To return to that vexing question of the virtual house: it seems to me that the virtual house may well be the house whose design incorporates whatever gadgets and technological features it desires (ranging from the megadigitalization involved in Bill Gates's house to the more mundane surveillance systems now readily incorporated in many homes and offices). The degree of its technologization is not a clear index of the degree of its openness to virtuality. If virtuality resides in the real (as the oxymoron "virtual reality" implies), this is because the real is always in fact open to the future, open to potentialities other than those now actualized. The challenge that VR poses to architecture cannot be reduced to the question of technology. If this occurs, then the question "How can this x (building, computer system, mode of simulation, structure of desire) function otherwise, open to difference?" is elided. And this is the crucial question that the virtual continually poses to the real: How can the real expand itself? The virtual poses no threat to the real because it is a mode of production and enhancement of the real: an augmentation, a supplementation, and a transformation of the real by and through its negotiation with virtuality.

Virtuality is not limited to the arena of technological innovation. Perhaps the most conventional of architectural forms and presumptions best illustrates what I understand as the impact, resonance, and richness that the virtual brings to the real: the wall. The capacity of walls, boxes, windows, and corners to function in more than one way, to serve not only present functions but others as well, is already part of the ingenuity and innovation of the virtual in the real. Makeshift, piecemeal transformations, the usage of spaces outside their conventional functions, the possibility of being otherwise—that is, of becoming—must be as readily accorded to the built environment as it is to all futurity.

1. In-Between

What does it mean to reflect upon a position, a relation, a place related to other places but with no place of its own: the position of the in-between? The in-between is a strange space, not unlike the choric space that Plato, in the *Timaeus,* posed as the condition of all material existence. For Plato, chora is that which, lacking any substance or identity of its own, falls in between the ideal and the material; it is the receptacle or nurse that brings matter into being, without being material; it nurtures the idea into its material form, without being ideal. The position of the in-between lacks a fundamental identity, lacks a form, a givenness, a nature. Yet it is that which facilitates, allows into being, all identities, all matter, all substance. It is itself a strange becoming, which is somehow, very mysteriously in Plato, the condition of all beings and the mediation of Being. There is a certain delicious irony in being encouraged to think about a strange and curious placement, a position that is crucial to understanding not only identities, but also that which subtends and undermines them, which makes identities both possible and impossible. The space of the in-between is that which is not a space, a space without boundaries of its own, which takes on and receives itself, its form, from the outside, which is not *its* outside (this would imply that it has a form) but whose form is the outside of the identity, not just of an other (for that would reduce the in-between to the role of object, not of space) but of others, whose relations of positivity define, by default, the space that is constituted as in-between.

The space of the in-between is the locus for social, cultural, and natural transformations: it is not simply a convenient space for movements and realignments but in fact is the only place—the place around identities, between identities—where becoming, openness to futurity, outstrips the conservational impetus to retain cohesion and unity. My argument will deal explicitly with the implications of what might be described as a posthumanist understanding of temporality and identity, an understanding that is bound up with seeing politics, movement, change, as well as space and time, in terms of the transformation and realignment of the relations between identities and elements rather than in terms of the identities, intentions, or interiorities of the wills of individuals or groups. An openness to futurity is the challenge facing all of the arts, sciences, and humanities; the degree of openness is an index of one's political alignments and orientations, of the readiness to transform. Unless we put into question architectural and cultural identities—the identities of men and women, of different races and classes, and of different religious, sexual, and political affiliations, as well as the identities of cities, urban regions, buildings, and houses—this openness to the future, the promise of time unfolding through innovation rather than prediction, is muted rather than welcomed.

The in-between has been a privileged concept for only a short time, for only in the last century or less has it been understood as a space or a positivity at all, as something more than a mere residue or inevitable consequence of other interactions. The first great thinker of the in-between is probably Henri Bergson, for whom the question of becoming, the arc of movement, is the most central frame. Instead of conceiving of relations between fixed identities, between entities or things that are only externally bound, the in-between is the only space of movement, of development or becoming: the in-between defines the space of a certain virtuality, a potential that always threatens to disrupt the operations of the identities that constitute it. The model of an in-betweenness, of an indeterminacy or undecidability, pervades the writings of contemporary philosophers, including Deleuze, Derrida, Serres, and Irigaray, where it goes under a number of different names: difference, repetition, iteration, the interval, among others. The space in between things is the space in which things are undone, the space to the side and around, which is the space of subversion and fraying, the edges of any identity's limits. In short, it is the space of the bounding and undoing of the identities which constitute it.

For this reason, the in-between has become a celebrated and prolific metaphor for many feminist and postmodern discourses, although it is rarely described as such. This in-between is the very site for the contestation of the many binaries and dualisms that dominate Western knowledge, for the very form of oppositional structure that has defined not only phallocentrism but also ethnocentrism and Eurocentrism, and the more general erasure of difference. The dualization of reality, the imposition of a representational structure that confirms the logic of self-identity—also known as the logic of the *excluded middle*—is one of the preeminent strategies in the propagation of power relations at the level of epistemology. In a structure of rigid polar oppositions—oppositions that are mutually exclusive and mutually exhaustive (A and –A)—the slash, the imperceptible line dividing the A from the –A, one binary term from its other, is the place of the excluded middle, the only space of negotiation between them, the only room to move, the only position from which to insinuate a rift or hole into the self-defined term that establishes binary privilege, and thus into the orbit of the binary structure itself. Irigaray, for example, has shown that the logic of dualisms involves not two terms but only the semblance of two terms. Phallocentrism is the use of a neutral or universal term to define both sexes: within this structure, there is not one term, *man*, and another independent term that is denigrated, *woman*. Rather, there is only one term, the other being defined as what it is not, its other or opposite. Irigaray's claim is that woman is erased as such within this logic: there is no space for women because taking their place is the specter or simulacrum of woman, man's fanciful counterpart, that which he has expelled and othered from himself. There is no woman in this structure, only the formula of a woman that would complement, supplement, and privilege masculinity. Similarly, in the structures of ethnocentrism and Eurocentrism, there is no other who exists independent of the self-same or sovereign subject who always *defines* the other only in its own image.

The in-between is what fosters and enables the other's transition from being the other of the one to its own becoming, to reconstituting another relation, in different terms. This in-between is that which is thus shared by politics, by culture, and by architecture, insofar as they are all spaces, organizations, structures, that operate within the logic of identity yet also require the *excess* of subversion, of latency, or of becoming that generates and welcomes the new without which the future is not possible. The in-between, formed by juxtapositions and experiments, formed by realignments or new arrangements, threatens to open itself up as new, to facilitate transformations in the identities that constitute it. One could say that the in-between is the locus of futurity, movement, speed; it is thoroughly spatial and temporal, the very essence of space and time and their intrication. And thus inimical to the project of architecture as a whole.

Gilles Deleuze is certainly the most self-proclaimed theorist of the in-between, which he describes in terms of the middle: his dictum is to proceed from the middle, to make connections not according to genealogy or teleology, but according to networks of movement and force. I want to turn now to some Deleuzian concepts in order to explore the contesting of the identities of culture and architecture that we are asked to position ourselves in between. Deleuze's work allows us to question the very ideal of "constructing an identity": he enables us to bypass the presumption that such an identity is necessary, or desirable, for the ongoing well-being of subjects and cultures. Or rather, his work affirms that any identity is always riven with forces, with processes, connections, movements that exceed and transform identity and that connect individuals (human and nonhuman) to each other and to worlds, in ways unforeseen by consciousness and unconnected to identity. In the work of Deleuze, Irigaray, or Derrida, or for that matter in postmodern or posthuman discourses more generally, this question of the excess that simultaneously conditions and undermines identity is commonly identified as the question of *difference*. The concept of difference is another mode of formulating questions of becoming, futurity, betweenness, and thus a way of problematizing conceptions of being, identity, and self-presence that dominate both thought and building in the present. (It is significant that Deleuze, Derrida, and Irigaray each specify that difference "has" an irreducible relation to the conceptualization of space and time: difference is not simply the collapsing [or circulation] of identity, it is also the rendering of space and time as fragmented, transformable, interpenetrated, beyond any fixed formulation, no longer guaranteed by the a priori or by the universalisms of science.)

2. Nature: Architecture and Culture's Becoming

Implicit in the pervasiveness of structures of binarization is the refusal to acknowledge the invisibility or negligibility of the subordinated term, its fundamental erasure as an autonomous or contained term. The binary structure not only defines the privileged term as the only term of the pair, but it infinitizes the negative term, rendering it definitionally amorphous, the receptacle of all that is excessive or expelled from the circuit of the privileged term. Yet while attempting to definitively and definitionally anchor terms, while struggling for a settled, stabilized power relation, while presenting themselves as immutable and given, dualisms are always in the process of subtle renegotiation and redefinition. They are considerably more flexible in their scope and history than their logic would indicate, for each term shifts and their values realign, while the binarized structure remains intact. In architecture, among the more relevant of these oppositional pairs are form and content, site and design, plan and construction, ornament and structure; in the field of cultural studies, the most relevant pairs include the oppositions between nature and culture, diachrony and synchrony, immanence and transcendence, same and other. Contesting schools or positions will uphold one or the other of these terms, such as nature or culture, or will propose a merger, which incorporates elements of one of the terms according to the logic of the other—for example, a nature-oriented or -friendly culture, a culture in tune with the natural—but which nonetheless leaves the binary structure itself unquestioned and fully functional. It would be a mistake to assume that these oppositional categories are somehow fixed or immune to reordering and subtle shifts. For example, where *nature* has tended to remain the ignored and denigrated term in both cultural and architectural studies, it has also, not too long ago, functioned as the privileged term. It has, in effect, reversed positions with its other, *culture*, as the privileged and defining term of the polarized pair: nature is now regarded as that residue either left over from or unassimilable to the cultural. It is now nature that is defined through its opposition to what is conceived of as culture, that is, the negation or residue left over from the cultural, its cultural waste.

Much feminist and postmodern discourse has been based on this apparently definitive renunciation of the category of the natural. The elevation of culture and the social to the privileged object of intellectual analysis has occurred partly as the result of the denigration and expulsion of the natural from the humanities and partly as a result of the apparently increasing control that the natural sciences seem to have over their "natural" objects of investigation. Nature, in cultural and architectural discourses, is conceived either as a passive, inert, ahistorical burden—in architecture, the burden of site specificity or the natural limit of materials—or else as a romanticized refuge or haven from the cultural, a cultural invention for its own recuperatively included "outside." Ironically, this is as true for philosophy and cultural studies as it is for architecture: they have all participated in the ever more firm opposition between the natural and the cultural, rewriting the natural as the dissimulated product or effect of culture, the cultural production or inscription of nature. This strategy may well have been initiated as a mode of political reversal of the privilege granted to the natural in the discourses articulating relations of race, class, and sex, but it has now succeeded in banishing the natural to the category of irrelevance, to the ever-shrinking real that is produced, inscribed, and contained by the frame of the symbolic and the imaginary, that is, the frame of culture. Nature becomes the repository of what must be overcome, transcended, reinscribed in culture's image, and thereby forbidden as ground or as matter, ejected as constraint, and refused as positivity or impetus. In a certain sense, it is nature that falls into the space "between" or before the juxtaposition and coincidence of the urban, the architectural, and the cultural. Nature is the other of these terms, the space in between them and the condition of their possibility and the impetus for their self-overcoming.

I am not interested in affirming a fixed, static nature, either: the limits of any fixed, deterministic naturalism have been made apparent over the last twenty years or more. Instead, I am interested in rethinking the status of the natural, to affirm it and to grant it the openness to account for the very inception of culture itself. Nature must be understood in the rich and productive openness attributed to it by Darwin and evolutionary theory, by Nietzsche, Deleuze, or Simondon, as force, as production, as a revelry in the random and the contingent, as a continuous opening up to the unexpected, as relations of dissonance, resonance, and consonance as much as relations of substance or identity. Rather than seeing it as either fixed origin, given limit, or predetermined goal, nature, the natural, must be seen as the site and locus of impetus and force, the ground of a malleable materiality, whose plasticity and openness account for the rich variability of cultural life, *and* the various subversions of cultural life that continue to enrich it. The natural must be understood as fundamentally open to history, to transformation, or to becoming, as open as culture, as innovative, temporal, and historical as the purview of social, psychical, and cultural life. The natural is the domain of bodies, the domain of materiality, which is not to suggest that bodies and materiality are thereby somehow outside of culture. These bodies are natural, but to say this is in no way to limit them: nature is the resource for all bodies, whether microscopic, middle-sized, or macroscopic. Bodies are the debt that culture owes to nature, the matter, attributes, energies, the forces it must make and make over as its own.

It is significant that among the more relevant discourses for understanding identity are those coming from apparently the most inert of natural studies, geology and crystallography, which have been so influential in the work of Deleuze and Guattari, especially in *A Thousand Plateaus*. Much recent work has regarded processes of individuation, not in terms of identities or substance, but in terms of a series of states of metastable equilibrium, and thus irreducibly in terms of processes of becoming. Simondon may have succeeded in going a step further than Bergson in thinking the implications of movement as the internal condition of individuation or being itself. To Simondon, individuation is a series of processes of radical excentering and self-exceeding (even at the nonorganic level of the crystal):

The concept of being that I put forward, then, is the following: a being does not possess a unity in its identity, which is that of the stable state within which no transformation is possible; rather, a being has a transductive unity, that is, it can pass out of phase with itself, it can—in any arena—break its own bounds in relation to its center. What one assumes to be a relation or a duality of principles is in fact the unfolding of the being, which is more than a unity and more than an identity; becoming is a dimension of the being, not something that happens to it following a succession of events that affect a being already and originally given and substantial. Individuation must be grasped as the becoming of the being and not as a model of the being which would exhaust his signification. . . . Instead of presupposing the existence of substances in order to account for individuation, I intend, on the contrary, to take the different regimes of individuation as providing the foundation for different domains such as matter, life, mind and society.[1]

To the extent that I affirm the centrality of nature to any understanding of culture and architecture, I also thus affirm the centrality of bodies—human and nonhuman, living and nonorganic—to formulating and refiguring an understanding of the in-between separating and linking architecture and culture. It is the interaction, arrangement, and regulation of such bodies that constitute the domains of both the architectural and the cultural. I have written elsewhere of the co-implication of bodies and cities, their relations of mutual production and definition;[2] here I want to focus more closely on that which renders any notion of identity, of a concordance between the projects of architecture and cultural enlightenment, impossible. I want to view nature—that is to say, materiality in time, materiality whose only destination is futurity, openness, and endless ramification—as the undoing of the aspirations of art and culture (which come together in unique form as architecture) to stability, identity, progress.

Nature is the stuff of culture and thus of architecture. Which is not to say that culture and architecture are nothing but natural: they are the consequences of the endless ramifications, intertwinings, and openness of the natural to all modes of manipulation, nature's open-ended completion by architecture, the landscape's fundamental openness to architectural rewriting. Architecture constitutes a raw interface between/as the cultural and the natural: its task, among other things, is the negotiation between a nature that poses itself as resistance and a culture that represents itself as limit. In short, architecture must negotiate between, on the one hand, cognizance and reshaping of the site, the organization and structuring of building materials, the development of a design that acknowledges or poses questions for these "resources" (nature here tends to function as "standing reserve," ready at hand), and on the other hand the cultural and economic exigencies that commission and inhabit architectural constructions. Architecture is a kind of probe that seeks out and remakes geological and geographic formations while being directed by the requirements of an aesthetic, economic, corporate, and engineering amalgam. Whereas the cultural factors motivating architectural design and practice—the structure of the competitive or jury process, the economic limits imposed on all building construction, the aesthetic and intellectual training of architects—have long been subject to analysis, it is less usual to explore how architectural discourse and practice are invested in and committed to a particular conception of the natural.

Architecture thus always borders on a nature that is often not acknowledged as such: indeed, the more we concentrate on architecture's position within a cultural context, the more we obscure the very peculiar nature on which it also relies. This is a nature that is open equally to intensive or extensive multiplicities, to numerical division or cohesion, to movements that are as open to the unpredictable as they are driven by the forces of determinism, that are as amenable to the grinding criteria of repeatability as they are experimental transformations and moments of unique and unrepeatable singularity. Architecture relies on a double nature—nature as standing reserve, as material to be exploited and rewritten, but also a nature that is always the supersession and transformation of limits and thus beyond the passivity of the reserve or the resource, nature as becoming or evolution.

This concept of nature is not simply the limit-condition of architecture or of the arts of engineering, exploration, and construction that come face-to-face with the resistance of the real, but also defines the limits and boundaries of culture, culture understood as contiguous with the social order, understood as the productive excess of the natural. This culture, the polar opposite of an inert

nature, also relies on the excessive permutations and ramifications of a nature that is not made up of laws in any ju-
dicial or regulative sense but rather of principles, vectors,
movements, trajectories, modes of openness to an unpredictable future. It is not coincidental that the statistical
mappings of cultural and economic relations closely follow the statistical structures of animal and organic evolution, and that computer simulations of social and natural
populations have a remarkably similar degree of accuracy.[3]
The cultural—the sphere of personal and social identity
and their transformation—can only function in its openness to history and contingency through the openness to
becoming entailed by a cultural evolution that is part of
and functions as an extension of biological evolution. Evolution is evolution, and its openness functions as such,
whether it is cultural or natural.

3. Power and the In-Between

Power has been understood in a variety of ways: as a coer-
cive force, as a rule by law or by a majority or the strongest,
as a weight of prohibition or the force of proliferation. In
his later, genealogical writings, Foucault demonstrated
that if power is to function as a mode of coercion and constraint, it can do so only through the establishment of mi-
crolinkages, capillary relations, relations that are primarily
productive, enabling, positive. In a certain sense, Foucault's work on power can be seen as the culmination or ex-
plication of an account of power that links it to becoming
and difference, to evolution and futurity (it is significant
that he never refers to Darwin in his writings). Power is
what proliferates, and its proliferation in a particular sce-
nario is contingent on its ability to overcome or absorb
obstacles in its path, to use them as part of its own self-
overcoming. Power, in short, is force directed to securing
a future in the face of its inherent openness. The relation

of power and futurity is paradoxical in that power recognizes the need for a most thorough anticipation of future trends or directions, but must nevertheless abandon itself to the force or pull of a future that it cannot secure and which may, at any moment, serve to reverse its thrust.

Culture and architecture are part of the field on which power relations play themselves out. While no more the province of power than any other social activity, the sphere of cultural production, within which architecture must also be located, is not neutral with respect to various alignments of power: the more congealed, formulaic, predictable, and recognizable the cultural and architectural forms, the more they aim at conserving a facet of the past and reducing the future to a form of its repetition. In spite of its place in the rhetoric of radical politics since Hegel, recognition is the force of conservation, the tying of the new and the never-conceived to that which is already cognized. History is itself the record of the workings of dominant social groups and categories, even though it also contains the traces of alternative forces and movements, virtualities whose force is yet to come or perhaps will never be. The history of these repressed, submerged, or half-articulated forces and events—those left behind in Hegelian sublation (in this sense, Hegel is the antithesis of Darwin!)—cannot be written with the same ease, readiness, and language available to canonical histories. The history of culture, and the history of architecture within it, is the playing out of these forces of actualization and realization at different rates of development, which themselves are functions of power investments.

The overlapping fields of architecture and culture, which congeal identities—the identities of individuals as subjects, as sexes, races, classes, but also the identity of movements and groups (political, professional, stylistic)—are also sites for the unhinging of identities and the initiation of pathways of self-overcoming: in Deleuzian terms, "in all things, there are lines of articulation or segmentarity, strata and territories; but also lines of flight, movements of deterritorialization and destratification."[4] In short, to the same degree that a certain subjective, symbolic, and psychical cohesion—the cohesion required by and produced for stable identity, whether cultural or architectural—is possible at all (and it is considerably less secure than naturalisms may want to affirm), these same stabilized and congealed forces can be reanimated and revivified in another direction. This is not the abolition of history or a refusal to recognize the past and the historical debt the present owes to it, but simply to refuse to grant even the past the status of fixity and givenness. The past is always contingent on what the future makes of it.

The history of architecture, as much as the history of culture, is the unpredictable opening out of forms, materials, practices, and arrangements; it is the dissemination, and thus the deformation and deviation, of norms, ideals, and goals that were once taken as given or unquestionable. Power relations are subject to the laws of iteration or futurity: they function and remain cohesive only to the extent that they repeat themselves and congeal over time, retaining a fundamental identity even amidst ever-changing details. Power relations, like matter and like life, are dissipative structures that also exercise chaotic bursts, upheavals, derangements, reorganization, quantum leaps. Insofar as they retain any identity, they also continually transform themselves, while nonetheless clinging to the goal of freezing, arresting, or containing the future in its own image and according to its own interests.

This force of futurity, which regulates the technological self-supersession that has marked historical moments in architectural and cultural life (as seen in the endless reflections on how computing technologies affect interpersonal, social, and cultural relations, as well as architectural practices at the conception, designing, and construction phases), is that debt to or reliance on the natural that neither contemporary cultural studies nor architectural discourses are capable of acknowledging. For it is this force of nature—not nature as ground, as matter, as standing reserve or resource—that is most significant in our understandings of cultural, social, and psychical life, life which is lived and immersed architecturally, aesthetically, ethically, and politically. That in nature which partakes of self-overcoming, of the random, the contingent, the unexpected, mutation—in short, the irreducible immersion of matter in space and time, in extension and becoming—has been elided for too long in our thinking about cultural and social space. Nature does not provide either a ground or a limit to human or cultural activity: nature is what inhabits cultural life to make it dynamic, to make it grow and be capable of reorienting itself despite the desire of forms of power to fix or freeze this movement toward the future. The most dynamic elements of architecture, as well as those of the arts and social and political life, aspire to revel in the sheer thrill of the unknown: it is these dynamic—or perhaps we should say experimental (more in the artistic than scientific sense)—forces that enliven culture and all cultural production.

Part Three *Future Spaces*

Philosophy

What can philosophy bring to architectural discourse and its practice (the practices of design, cost analysis, siting, building)? And what can architecture bring to philosophical discourse and its practices (reasoning, arguing, formulating problematics, framing questions)? What are some pertinent points of overlap or mutual investment that may implicate each in the other in mutually productive ways? Perhaps more pertinently, what are the blind spots within the self-understanding of each? And how can each be used by the other, not just to affirm itself and receive external approval but also to question and thus to expand itself, to become otherwise, without assuming any privilege or primacy of the one over the other and without assuming that the relation between them must be one of direct utility or translation? One very small strand draws these two disciplines together: an idea of newness or virtuality, latency or becoming, which may be highlighted and productively developed within both disciplines through the help, the overlap, and the difference that each offers the other. This idea of the virtual, a concept prevalent if undeveloped in philosophy since at least the time of Plato, introduces a series of questions to both architecture and philosophy (with different effects) that may force them to change quite fundamental assumptions they make about space, time, movement, futurity, and becoming.

Architecture has tended to conceive of itself as an art, a science, or a mechanics for the manipulation of space, indeed probably the largest, most systematic and most powerful mode for spatial organization and modification. Space itself, the very stuff of architectural reflection and production, requires and entails a mode of time, timeliness, or duration. Indeed, space must always involve at least two times, or perhaps two kinds of time. The first is the time of the emergence of space as such, a time before time and space, a temporalization/spatialization that precedes and renders the organization or emergence of space as such and time as such and thus emerges before any scientific understanding of a space-time continuum.[1] This is the space-time of difference, of *différance* (Jacques Derrida discusses *différance* as precisely the temporization of space and the spatialization of time), or differentiation (in Deleuzian terms, differing from itself), which is a precondition of and prior to the space and time of life, of understanding, of science.

Derrida, for example, claims that the insertion of an interval that refuses self-identity and self-presence to any thing, any existent, constitutes *différance*. This interval, neither clearly space nor time but a kind of leakage between the two, the passage of the one into the other, propels any being beyond itself, in space and in time. Neither space nor time can exist as such "before" this interval, which expands being into a world in order that it paradoxically be both itself and other to itself:

An interval must separate the present from what it is not in order for the present to be itself but this interval that constitutes it as present must, by the same token, divide the present in and of itself, thereby also dividing, along with the present, everything that is thought on the basis of the present, that is, in our metaphysical language, every being, and singularly substance or the subject. In constituting itself, in dividing itself dynamically, this interval is what might be called *spacing*, the becoming-space of time or the becoming-time of space (*temporization*). And it is this constitution of the present, as an "originary" and irreducibly nonsimple . . . synthesis of marks, or traces of retentions and protentions . . . that I propose to call archi-writing, archi-trace, or *différance*. Which (is) (simultaneously) spacing (and) temporization.[2]

The time and space of architecture, and for that matter, of philosophy, can rarely afford to consider this primordial differential, the movement, the shimmering of the differing of a time and space not yet configured, enumerated, mastered, or occupied. This time before time, the time of the interval, the time of nontime, enables space to emerge as such and is that to which space is ineluctably driven, the "fate" of space.

There is a second kind of time, the time of history, of historicity, the time of reflection, the time of knowledge— a time to which we are accustomed in the history of architecture and of philosophy in the very idea of history, of orderly progression, of the segmentation or continuity of time and space. Architecture has tended to face time and temporality through the questions posed by history and through its response to the ravages of that history, its orientation toward monumentality. Architecture has thought time, with notable exceptions, through history rather than through duration, as that to be preserved, as that which somehow or provisionally overcomes time by transcending or freezing it.

I am more interested here in the relevance of the first sense of time, which I will represent through the concept of the virtual and virtuality, a concept that requires not only a time *before* time but also a time *after* time, a time bound up not only with the past and with history and historicity but also, perhaps primarily, with futurity, thus providing a mode of resistance to the privilege of the present and the stranglehold that the present and its correlatives, identity and intention, maintain on space and matter. The times before and after time are the loci of emergence, of unfolding, of eruption, the spaces-times of the new, the unthought, the virtuality of a past that has not exhausted itself in activity and a future that cannot be exhausted or anticipated by the present. This past, which layers and resonates the present, refuses to allow the present the stability of the given or the inevitable. It is the past that enables duration as a mode of continuity as well as heterogeneity. Both Derrida and Deleuze, in very different ways, indicate this central role of difference as a vector in the modalization of space.

In articulating a notion of virtuality linked to futurity, to becoming and to differentiation, I want to explicate what I understand as a particularly underrepresented philosophical mode, which philosophy may share with architecture, what might be called a "logic of invention" as opposed to an Aristotelian logic of identity, reflection, reason, self-containment. A logic of invention has yet to be invented: only such a logic can mediate between the reflective categories of philosophical thought and the pragmatic requirements of any empirical project, here the architectural project. It is a linkage that invents new philosophies and new architectures. Instead of the self-containment of the syllogism (in which conclusions are logically entailed in validly constituted premises), a logic of invention is necessarily expansive, ramifying, and expedient, producing not premises so much as techniques, not conclusions so much as solutions, not arguments so much as effects. Such a logic can never be regulative (distinguishing valid from invalid arguments) but is always descriptive (do this, then this, then this).

Philosophy, according to Deleuze, is both a mode of solving problems and a mode of thinking or theorizing multiplicities. Architecture too is bound up with problem solving and with multiplicities, though the multiplicities with which it deals are not simply conceptual or simply material. Philosophy is not, for Deleuze, a mode of mastering the real, framing its rules, understanding its principles; rather, it is what deals with the coagulation, the alignments between the actual and the virtual, the ways in which the actual feeds off and grows in distinction from the virtual and, conversely, the ways in which the virtual continually enriches and diminishes the actual by forcing it to diverge from itself, to always tend toward and to be absorbed by virtuality. Architecture, like philosophy (and for that matter, biology and physics), is perpetually verging on, irresistibly drawn to, its own virtualities, to the ever-increasing loops of uncertainty and immanence that its own practices engage and produce. The future of each discipline requires that each open itself up to a reconsideration of the virtual and the promise it holds for newness, otherness, divergence from what currently prevails.

What does the notion of the virtual mean? Here I only have the time (or is it the space!) to deal with one conception in any detail, Deleuze's reading of Bergson, and Bergson's understanding of the virtual and the return of the virtual image to the actual. Deleuze claims that Bergson is one of the great thinkers of becoming, of duration, multiplicity, and virtuality. Bergson developed his notion of duration in opposition to his understanding of space and spatiality. This understanding of duration and the unhinging of temporality that it performs are of at least indirect relevance to the arts or sciences of space, which may, through a logic of invention, derail and transform space and spatiality in analogous ways.

Space is understood, according to Deleuze (who follows Bergson at least up to a point on this), as a multiplicity that brings together the key characteristics of externality, simultaneity, contiguity or juxtaposition, differences of degree, and quantitative differentiations.

Space is discontinuous, infinitely divisible, static, and always actual. Space in short is the milieu of things, matter, identities, substances, entities that are real, comparable, and calculable. It is the natural home of science, of the actual, where there are differentiations of degree but not in kind:

> Space, by definition, is outside us . . . space appears to us to subsist even when we leave it undivided, we know that it can wait and that a new effort of our imagination may decompose it when we choose. As, moreover, it never ceases to be space, it always implies juxtaposition, and, consequently, possible division. Abstract space is, indeed, at bottom, nothing but the mental diagram of infinite divisibility.[3]

Duration, by contrast, is a multiplicity of succession, heterogeneity, differences in kind and qualitative differentiations. It is continuous and virtual. Duration is divisible, of course, but it is transformed through the act of division—indeed, much of Bergson's work explores the implications of dividing time, among the more serious of which is the freezing of all motion into discrete momentary units. Duration is perfectly capable of subsisting without division, which is always imposed on it from the outside. Duration is not, through its continuity, homogeneous, smooth, or linear; rather, it is a mode of "hesitation," bifurcation, unfolding, or emergence.

If space and time are represented as discrete phenomena, as separate and indeed opposed, in their various qualities and attributes, then not only are these primordial processes of temporization that induce space ignored, but the primitive processes of spatialization through which the notion of duration and temporality exists also fail to emerge. Bergson himself acknowledges this, though only rarely, when he qualifies and refines his understanding of space. It is not that space in itself must be or can only be the space of quantification; rather, it is a certain mode of doing science, particularly science under the determinist, predictive Laplacian model, that effects the mathematization and ordering of space and makes this seem to be the very nature of space itself. In a certain sense Bergson acknowledges the becoming one of the other, the relation of direct inversion between them, when he conceptualizes space as the contraction of time, and time as the expansion or dilation of space.

Space is mired in misconceptions and assumptions, habits and unreflective gestures that convert and transform it. Architecture, the art or science of spatial manipulation, must be as implicated in this as any other discipline or practice. According to Bergson, a certain habit of thought inverts the relations between space and objects, space and extension, to make it seem as if space precedes objects, when in fact space itself is produced *through* matter, extension, and movement:

Concrete extensity, that is to say, the diversity of sensible qualities, is not within space; rather it is space that we thrust into extensity. Space is not a ground on which real motion is posited; rather it is real motion that deposits space beneath itself. But our imagination, which is preoccupied above all by the convenience of expression and the exigencies of material life, prefers to invert the natural order of the terms. . . . Therefore, it comes to see movement as only a variation of distance, space being thus supposed to precede motion. Then, in a space which is homogeneous and infinitely divisible, we draw, in imagination, a trajectory and fix positions: afterwards, applying the movement to the trajectory, we see it divisible like the line we have drawn, and equally denuded of quality.[4]

Space in itself, space outside these ruses of the imagination, is not static, fixed, infinitely expandable, infinitely divisible, concrete, extended, continuous, and homogenous, though perhaps we must think it in these terms in order to continue our everyday lives (and the architect is perhaps more invested in this understanding of space than anyone else). Space, like time, is emergence and eruption, oriented not to the ordered, the controlled, the static, but to the event, to movement or action. If we "shut up motion in space," as Bergson suggests, then we shut space up in quantification, without ever being able to think space in terms of quality, of difference and discontinuity. We do not think of space*s* but can at best allow ourselves to utter "places," in a gesture to localization. Space seems to resist this kind of pluralization: it asserts itself as continuous, singular, and infinite. Space presents itself as ready-made, as given in its constancy, fixed in its form: it is then a mode of the capture of both space and time when time is understood as the fourth dimension of space common in post-Einsteinian ontology.

It is relevant that Bergson calls for a space, or spaces, sensitive to the motion and actions that unfold in them. Rather than seeing motion in its scientific terms as distance or space over time, Bergson indicates, though he does not develop, a different understanding, where space emerges through specific motions and specific spaces, where motion unfolds and actualizes space. As Deleuze explains,

Space, in effect, is matter or extension, but the "schema" of matter, that is, the representation of the limit where the movement of expansion would come to an end as the external envelope of all possible extensions. In this sense, it is not matter, it is not extensity, that is in space, but the very opposite. And if we think that matter has a thousand ways of becoming expanded or extended, we must also say that there are all kinds of distinct extensities, all related, but still qualified, and which will finish by intermingling only in our own schema of space.[5]

This kind of space can no longer be considered static, infinitely extended, smooth, regular, amenable to gridding, to coordinates, to geometric division, the kind of space one can leave behind and return to intact, independent of what has occurred there. In opening up space to time, space becomes amenable to transformation and refiguring; it becomes particular, individualized. It is not clear that we need to return, as Bergson suggests, to the space of immediate, lived experience. For one thing, our lived experience at the end of the millennium involves spaces that were quite literally unimaginable in Bergson's time, and moreover, the immediacy of experience is itself not uninvested by the social modes of inhabitation of space. For another, it is not clear that immediate experience is any more the point of proliferation of virtualities and intensities than, say, the most intensely artificial and manufactured movements and spaces.

In a rare moment, Bergson contemplates the possibility of thinking space otherwise, understanding it in terms other than as the binary opposite of duration. Instead of being the pure medium of actuality, space too can be conceived as the field for the play of virtualities:

In regard to concrete extension, continuous, diversified and at the same time organized, we do not see why it should be bound up with the amorphous and inert space which subtends it—a space which we divide indefinitely, out of which we carve figures arbitrarily, and in which movement itself . . . can only appear as a multiplicity of instantaneous positions, since nothing there can ensure the coherence of past with present. It might, then, be possible, in a certain measure, to transcend space without stepping out from extensity; and here we should really have a return to the immediate, since we do indeed perceive extensity, whereas space is merely conceived—being a kind of mental diagram.[6]

Bergson suggests that we can reinvent, or rather, return to a conception of space that does not so much underlie or subtend matter, functioning as the indifferent coordinates of the placement of matter, as function as an effect of matter and movement. It is not an existing, God-given space, the Cartesian space of numerical division, but an unfolding space, defined, as time is, by the arc of movement and thus a space open to becoming, by which I mean becoming other than itself, other than what it has been:

If we try to get back to the bottom of this common hypothesis [shared by philosophical realism and idealism] . . . we find that it consists in attributing to homogeneous space a disinterested office: space is supposed either merely to uphold material reality or to have the function, still purely speculative, of furnishing sensations with means of coordinating themselves. So the obscurity of realism, like that of idealism, comes from the fact that, in both of them, our conscious perception and the conditions of our conscious perception are assumed to point to pure knowledge, not to action. But now suppose that this homogeneous space is not logically anterior, but posterior to material things and to the pure knowledge which we can have of them; suppose that extensity is prior to space; suppose that homogeneous space concerns our action and only our action, being like an infinitely fine network which we stretch beneath material continuity in order to render ourselves masters of it, to decompose it according to the plan of our activities and our needs. Then . . . our hypothesis [has] the advantage of bringing us into harmony with science, which shows us each thing exercising an influence on all the others and, consequently, occupying, in a certain sense, the whole of the extended.[7]

The same attributes of becoming that Bergson accords to duration can now be seen to accompany spatiality: just as the whole of the past contracts, in various degrees, in each moment of the present, that is, just as the present is laden with virtualities that extend it beyond itself—the ballast of the virtual past being enough to propel an unpredicted future out of an uncontained and endlessly ramifying present—so too the whole of space, spatiality, contracts into the specificity of location, and the occupation of any space contains the virtual whole of spatiality, which is to say, the infinite possibilities of my action on and being acted on by matter in space and time. To remember any moment is to throw oneself into the past, to seek events where they took place—in time, in the past; to experience any other space is to throw oneself into spatiality, to become spatialized with all of space. To remember (to place oneself in the past), to relocate (to cast oneself elsewhere), is to occupy the whole of time and the whole of space, even admitting that duration and location are always specific, always defined by movement and action. It is to refuse to conceptualize space as a medium, as a container, a passive receptacle whose form is given by its content, and instead to see it as a moment of becoming, of opening up and proliferation, a passage from one space to another, a space of change, which changes with time.

Instead of a return to the prescientific immediacy that Bergson suggests as a remedy for the containment that science places on space, I would suggest a different approach to the reenervation of space through duration, the restoration of becoming to both space and time. If time is neither linear and successive nor cyclical and recurrent but indeterminate, unfolding, serial, multiplying, complex, heterogeneous, then space too must be reconfigured not as neutral, nor as singular, and homogeneous but as opening up to other spaces, not regulating processes and events so much as accompanying them. We do not, as Bergson claims, need to *experience* or live such a space (or time): this does not seem possible or necessary. We need more adequately intellectual, but above all pragmatic, models by which to understand and actively seek the maximal paths of proliferation for virtual time becoming virtual space. These models are not simply modes of self-complacency that enable us to live our lives as before, now with a justification and a rationale; rather, these models may help us to understand, see, think, build differently, according to other logics of invention and experimentation.

Perceiving

To understand how the virtual may enrich conceptions of space and thus of the architectural project, we may need to make a brief detour through the role that the virtual plays in duration and especially in inserting the past into the present as its state of virtuality. This may in turn provide some of the key concepts or terms by which to think spatiality in terms of virtuality.

Bergson wants to define perception and memory, our modes of access to the present and the past, in operational or pragmatic terms: the present is that which acts, while the past can be understood as that which no longer acts or whose actions are at best virtual.[8] Perception must be linked to nascent or dawning action, action-in-potential. Perception is actual insofar as it is active and thus relates primarily to an impending future. By contrast, instead of memory being regarded as a faded perception, a perception that has receded into the past, as is commonplace, it must be regarded as ideational, inactive, virtual. "The past is only idea, the present is ideo-motor."[9] A present perception and a past recollection are not simply different in degree (one a faded, diminished version of the other) but different in kind. Perception is that which propels us toward the real, toward space, objects, matter, the future, while memory is that which impels us toward consciousness, the past, and duration.[10] If perception impels us toward action and thus toward objects, then, to that extent, objects reflect my body's possible actions upon them.

The present is that which acts and lives, that which functions to anticipate an immediate future in action. The present is a form of impending action. The past is that which no longer acts, although in a sense it lives a shadowy and fleeting existence. It still is. It is real. The past remains accessible in the form of recollections, either as motor mechanisms in the form of habit memory, or, more correctly, in the form of image memories. These memories are the condition of perception in the same way that the past, for Bergson, is a condition of the present. Whereas the past in itself is powerless, if it can link up to a present perception, it has a chance to be mobilized in the course of another perception's impulse to action. In this sense, the present is not purely self-contained; it straddles both past and present, requiring the past as its precondition, oriented as it is toward the immediate future. Our perception is a measure of our virtual action upon things. The present, as that which is oriented toward both perception and action, is the threshold of their interaction and thus the site of duration. The present consists in the consciousness I have of my body. Memory, the past, has no special link with or proximity to my body. Most significant for the purposes of this argument is that as the present functions in the domain of the actual, the past functions as virtual.

The past cannot be identified with the memory images that serve to represent or make it actual for or useful to us; rather, it is the seed that can actualize itself in a memory. Memory is the present's mode of access to the past. The past is preserved in time, while the memory image, one of the past's images or elements, can be selected according to present interests. Just as perception leads me toward objects where they are, outside of myself and in space, and just as I perceive affection (which Deleuze would refer to as intensity) where it arises, in my body,[11] so too I recall or remember only by placing myself in the realm of the past where memory subsides or subsists. Thus, paradoxically, memory, the past, is not *in us*, just as perception is not *in us*. Perception takes place outside ourselves, where objects are (in space); memory takes us to where the past is (in duration). In Deleuze's reading, Bergson goes so far as to say that the only subjectivity or life is time and that life participates in this subjectivity to the extent that it is submerged in duration.[12]

Bergson seems to problematize a whole series of assumptions regarding our conceptions of the present and the past. We tend to believe that when the present is exhausted or depleted of its current force, it somehow slips into the past where it is stored in the form of memories. It is then replaced by another present. Against this presumption, Bergson suggests that a new present could never replace the old one if the latter did not pass while it is still present. In place of the more usual claim of the succession of the past by the present, this leads to his postulate of the *simultaneity* of past and present. The past is contemporaneous with the present it has been. They exist, they "occur" at the same time. The past could never exist if it did not coexist with the present of which it is the past:

The past and the present do not denote two successive moments, but two elements which coexist: One is the present, which does not cease to pass, and the other is the past, which does not cease to be but through which all presents pass. . . . The past does not follow the present, but on the contrary, is presupposed by it as the pure condition without which it would not pass. In other words, each present goes back to itself as past.[13]

Bergson argues that the past would be altogether inaccessible to us if we can gain access to it only through the present and its passing. The only access we have to the past is through a leap into virtuality, through a move into the past itself, through seeing that the past is outside us and that we are in it rather than it in us. The past exists, but it is in a state of latency or virtuality. We must place ourselves in it if we are to have recollections, memory images. This we do in two movements or phases. First, we place ourselves into the past in general (which can only occur through a certain detachment from the immediacy of the present), and then we place ourselves in a particular region of the past. Bergson conceives of the past in terms of a series of planes or segments, each one representing the whole of the past in a more or less contracted form. We move from one set of memories to another through a leap into a virtual time. We must jump into the milieu of the past in general in order to access any particular memories. The present can be understood as an infinitely contracted moment of the past, the point where the past intersects most directly with the body. It is for this reason that the present is able to pass.

Each segment has its own features, although each contains within itself the whole of the past. Memories drawn from various strata may be clustered around idiosyncratic points, "shining points of memory," as Bergson describes them, which are multiplied to the extent that memory is dilated.[14] Depending on the recollection we are seeking, we must jump in at a particular segment; in order to move on to another, we must make another leap: "We have to jump into a chosen region, even if we have to return to the present in order to make another jump, if the recollection sought for gives no response and does not realize itself in a recollection-image."[15] For Deleuze, this provides a model for Bergson's understanding of our relations to other systems of images as well (and hence Bergson's suitability to Deleuze's analysis of cinema).

It is only through a similar structure that we can detach ourselves from the present to understand linguistic utterances or make conceptual linkages. The structure of the time image also contains that of the language image and the thought image. Only by throwing ourselves into language as a whole, into the domain of sense in general, can we understand any utterance, and only by leaping into a realm of ideas can we understand problems.[16] In all three cases, this leap involves landing in different concentrations of the past, language, or thought, which nonetheless contain the whole within them to different degrees.

Along with the simultaneity or coexistence of each moment of the present with the entirety of the past, there are other implications in Bergson's paradoxical account. Each moment carries a virtual past: each present must, as it were, pass through the whole of the past. This is what is meant by the past in general. The past does not come after the present has ceased to be, nor does the present become or somehow move into the past. Rather, it is the past which is the condition of the present; it is only through a preexistence that the present can come to be. Bergson does not want to deny that succession takes place—of course, one present (and past) replaces another—but such actual succession can only take place because of a virtual coexistence of the past and the present, the virtual coexistence of all of the past at each moment of the present—and at each level or segment of the past. Thus, there must be a relation of repetition between each segment whereby each segment or degree of contraction or dilation is a virtual repetition of the others, not identical, certainly, but a version. The degrees of contraction or dilation that differentiate segments constitute modes of repetition in difference.

In Deleuze's reading, Bergson systematically develops a series of paradoxes regarding the past and present that run counter to a more common, everyday understanding:

(1) we place ourselves at once, in a leap, in the ontological element of the past (paradox of the leap); (2) there is a difference in kind between the present and the past (paradox of Being); (3) the past does not follow the present that it has been, but coexists with it (paradox of coexistence); (4) what coexists with each present is the whole of the past, integrally, on various levels of contraction and relaxation (*détente*) (paradox of psychic repetition).

These Bergsonian paradoxes, which are only paradoxical if duration is represented on the model of space, are all, Deleuze claims, a critique of more ordinary theories of memory, whose propositions state that

(1) we can reconstitute the past with the present; (2) we pass gradually from the one to the other; (3) . . . they are distinguished by a before and an after; and (4) . . . the work of the mind is carried out by the addition of elements (rather than by changes of level, genuine jumps, the reworking of systems).[17]

It seems clear that a series of analogous unhingings of the self-containment and fixity of spatiality can also be developed, though Bergson himself refrains from doing so. Duration contains as part of its conceptual content the ideas of (1) unevenness, heterogeneity, states of contraction and expansion, such that time exists in a state of detailed elaboration or in a state of compressed schematism; (2) difference, specificity, and multiplicity: each movement has its own duration, each event its own unfolding. These durations, though, are never simply isolated or self-contained but always both intersect with other durations (the duration of my actions may interact with the durations of the objects and materials with which I work) and participate in a kind of megaduration, a world duration that renders them in a web or weave of comparable and interlocked durations and becomings; (3) simultaneity, the coexistence of the past in the present, the anticipation of the present as the actualization of the past (in other words, the coexistence of two kinds of time, one frozen and virtual, the other dynamic and actual). These two kinds of duration are irreducible in their difference: the past is contemporaneous with the present it has been; and (4) succession, the complication of the past, present, and future. Each is necessarily involved in the function of the others, not by way of determinism (which in fact annuls the existence of the future and enables the effectivity of the past only) but through the divergence of the present from the past, and the future from the present, the interlocking of the past and the future (both virtual, both productive without emerging as such through the present) without the mediation of the present.

These questions remain: Do these rather strange and paradoxical formulations of duration have any spatial counterparts? Can the ways in which we conceive, indeed live, space be subjected to a similar unhinging, a similar destabilization of presence and habitual self-evidence? To return to my earlier question: What would virtual space be like? What does such a conception entail? How can it be thought? How can it be built, lived, practiced?

I wrote above about the need for a logic of invention. Instead of requiring logical certainty, the guarantee of universal validity, the capacity to provide rules of procedure independent of the particularities of space and time, such a logic would instead require ingenuity, experimentation, novelty, specification, and particularity as its key ingredients. It would not seek to be certain but rather to incite, to induce, to proliferate. Rather than direct itself to questions of consistency, coherence, and regularity, such a logic would focus on an intuition of uniqueness, the facing of each situation according to its specific exigencies, the openness to failure as much as to innovation. I am not proposing that we replace Aristotelian logic with such a logic of invention; I only propose that we acknowledge that each may work and be relevant in its particular spheres. Such a "logic of invention" has always governed architecture. The question is: What are the best terms by which to articulate this logic? In other words, how can we extract its *own* theory from its architectural practices rather than simply import or impose a theoretical frame from the outside? This is to inquire about architecture's own (theoretical) latencies, its virtualities.

I can offer only a more general understanding of virtuality and what it implies for rethinking or perhaps reinventing space. I have two thoughts: one on the rethinking of space in terms of becoming and duration; the other on what the virtual can offer to architectural theory and practice.

To look, then, at some possibilities for the reconceptualization of space in terms of its openness to its own processes of differentiation and divergence. It seems possible that many—or at least some—of the qualities that Bergson attributes to duration may also be relevant to a considered spatiality, especially given that the time-space of primordial experience links space, before mathematization, to the movement of duration. Many of the attributes particular to duration may have some spatial equivalent. For example, if duration exists in states of contraction and expansion, in degrees of uneven intensity, either elaborated in increasing detail or functioning simply as "shining points" of intensity, then perhaps space too need not be construed as even, homogeneous, continuous, infinitely the same. Perhaps space also has loci of intensity, of compression or elasticity; perhaps it need no longer be considered a medium. Perhaps it can be considered lumpy, intensified, localized, or regionalized. I am not talking here simply of locale or landscape but also of the fundamental or ontological space that underlies a specific region. Nor am I simply confirming the insights of an Einsteinian space-time, in which there is still a relation of smooth, mathematical alignments between the expansion of time and the contraction of space. The very configurations of space itself may be heterogeneous, just as the movements or configurations of duration vary. Perhaps, in other words, there is a *materiality* to space itself, rather than materiality residing with only its contents.

This implies that space itself, if it is heterogeneous, is multiple, differential, specific. There are specific locations, places, regions that have their own modes of extensity: like intensity, the extensive always radiates from a point, given spatially as "here," the spatial present. The spatial present defines its own region, but this regionality both intersects with the regionality of other heres and, like world duration, links to a larger space, a world space or even a universal space, which in no way qualifies or marginalizes the concrete differences between different spaces. Cosmological spaces are not the master or overarching space within which places or regions are located in a mode of neutralization; cosmological space could itself be regarded as patchwork and uneven.

If two types of time coexist, one virtual (the past) and the other actual (the present) and their coexistence is necessary for the functioning of either, then perhaps there is a spatial correlate for this unhinging of temporal continuity through Bergson's paradoxical idea of the temporal simultaneity of present and past. Obviously, spatial relations happily admit relations of simultaneity: space is that which enables simultaneous or coextensive relations. Perhaps it would be more intriguing to consider spatiality in terms of the coexistence of multiple relations of *succession*, space as a layering of spaces within themselves, spaces enfolded in others, spaces that can function as the virtualities of the present, the "here." Here a notion of virtual space will be of crucial relevance. If past, present, and future are always entwined and make each other possible only through their divergences and bifurcations, then perhaps there is a way to consider spatiality in terms of relations of nearness and farness, relations of proximity and entwinement, the interimplications of the very near and the very far, rather than of numerals or geometry.

This possibility returns us once again to the vexing question of the virtual and its particular spatial resonances. One cannot of course directly specify what a virtual is, for insofar as it *is*, insofar as it exists, it exists as actual. In the process of actualization, the virtual annuls itself as such in order to reemerge as an actual that thereby produces its own virtualities. At best one can specify what the virtual may produce, what effects or differences it may generate. We need to remind ourselves of how Deleuze distinguishes between the virtual and the possible: he claims that the possible is the correlate or counterpart of the real. There are two distinctive connections between the possible and the real: the real both resembles the possible and is a limitation of the possible. The possible, or at least one of them, is a preformed real: the real is simply the coming into material form of this nonmaterial possible. The real is a mode of conformity with the possible, its plan or blueprint. Or equally, the possible is simply the retrospectively conceived past of the real. By contrast, the virtual is counterposed with the actual rather than the real (indeed the virtual has a reality without any actuality). The actual in no way resembles the virtual nor does it limit or select from the virtual. It is linked to the virtual through "difference or divergence and . . . creation":

It is difference that is primary in the process of actualization—the difference between the virtual from which we begin and the actuals at which we arrive, and also the difference between the complementary lines according to which actualization takes place. In short, the characteristic of virtuality is to exist in such a way that it is actualized by being differentiated and is forced to differentiate itself.[18]

Thus the virtual *requires* the actual to diverge, to differentiate itself, to proceed by way of division and disruption, forging modes of actualization that will transform this virtual into others unforeseen by or uncontained within it. In other words, virtuality functions evolutionarily: it functions through the production of the novelties that remain unforeseen by, yet somehow generated through, the virtual materials ("genes" or seeds). The virtual is the realm of productivity, of functioning otherwise than its plan or blueprint, functioning in excess of design and intention. This is the spark of the new that the virtual has over the possible: the capacity for generating innovation through an unpredicted leap, the capacity of the actual to be more than itself, to become other than the way it has always functioned. It is differentiation that, while propelled by a tendency or virtuality, can only actualize itself through its encounters with matter, with things, with movements and processes, and thus with obstacles, through which it produces itself as always other than its virtuality, always new, singular, and unique.[19]

How then can space function differently from the ways in which it has always functioned? What are the possibilities of inhabiting otherwise? Of being extended otherwise? Of living relations of nearness and farness differently?

How [can] a city engage in philosophy without being destroyed?

Plato, *The Republic*

What is realized in my history is not the past definite of what was, since it is no more, or even the present perfect of what has been in what I am, but the future anterior of what I shall have been for what I am in the process of becoming.

Jacques Lacan, *Écrits: A Selection*

The theme of embodied utopias provides me with the opportunity to explore some paradoxes or aporias, which are my favorite topic because they always imply a movement of systems—here systems of reason—beyond their own systematicity, and modes of containment that are unable to quite contain or control that which they draw into their circle of influence. The phrase "embodied utopias" itself hovers between terms that are tense and uneasy in their relations. It is this tension, especially when it expresses itself most acutely in the form of the paradoxical, that always provides the strongest motivations for rethinking categories, terms, and assumptions, and for adding complications to perhaps oversimplified frameworks within which those terms were thought. Utopias are the spaces of phantasmatically attainable political and personal ideals, the projection of idealized futures; embodiment, though, is that which has never had its place within utopias. It is not clear whether the phrase "embodied utopias" is an oxymoron or not! I want to look at the productive (and perhaps impossible) relations between utopias and embodiment, which link together some elements of architectural discourse and practice with the political and theoretical concerns of postmodern feminism. I believe that this amalgam of interests—feminist, political, architectural, corporeal—converges on a focal point that has tended to be elided in the history of Western thought: the question of time and futures. So although architecture will be my (perhaps too indirect) object, it will be time that will prove to be my subject.

The Utopic

Discourses of utopia have been with us since the advent of Western philosophy. Plato's *Republic* and *Laws*, which foreshadow Aristotle's *Politics*, provide the basis for the more modern forms that utopic discourses, those structured around ideal forms of political organization, will take in the West. What is significant, and bitterly ironic, about Plato's formulation of the ideal social and political organization is his understanding that the *polis*, a city-state, should be governed by philosopher-kings, should function under the domination of an order imposed by reason. Like the orderly body, the city-state functions most ably under the rule of reason, the regime of wisdom, for the well-ordered *polis*, like the well-ordered body, operates most harmoniously only in accordance with the dictates of pure reason and the contemplation of the eternal. This is the basis of Plato's claim that the guardians, rulers of the Republic, need to be those most skilled in reason and the love of truth, yet also tested in the world for their moral character. Their theoretical or abstract reason must be put to the test of worthy concrete practices: "No perfect city or constitution, and equally no perfect individual, would ever come to be until these philosophers, a few who are not wicked but are now said to be useless, are compelled by chance, whether they wish it or not, to take charge of the city and that city is compelled to obey them."[1]

More recognizable as a "modern" template of the utopic than the philosophical oligarchy Plato theorized should rule over the ideal republic is Thomas More's 1516 text *Utopia*, which is, among other things, as More himself describes it, a complex and ambivalent sixteenth-century "treatise on the best constitution of a republic."[2] Utopia is the name of an island, which comprises an insulated and relatively self-contained community, space, and economy, surrounded by a calm sea. Access to foreigners and especially invaders is difficult, for the Utopians are protected by a perilous and rocky harbor, which requires their navigational aid for ships to be safe, guaranteeing the island against the dangers of uninvited entry. The sea surrounding the island forms an inlet, an interior lake or harbor, a calm and windless space, surrounded and thus protected by dangerous rocks. The harbor inside the island reflects an internalized version of the sea surrounding it, almost like an interiorized mirror representation of its exterior. This calm, harmonious integration is exhibited not only in the climate and location, the geography, of Utopia, but also in its political organization, its devotion to solemn self-regulation, to the egalitarian distribution of goods, and to modesty, diligence, and virtue. Its geography complements, and perhaps enables, its political organization. If the calm harbor reflects the serenity of the sea, the sea functions as emblem of political harmony, for the Utopians live in the best form of commonwealth, though one with its own terrible costs: the intense constraints on personal freedom that seem characteristic of all social-contract theorists.

Long recognized as a perplexing and paradoxical enterprise, More's text, like Plato's, involves the postulate of a rationally organized society, which is fundamentally egalitarian in organization,[3] being founded on the notion of communal, rather than private, property and collective, rather than individual, self-interest. This ideal commonwealth, which many claim anticipated the modern welfare state, is also, perhaps by necessity, rigidly authoritarian, hierarchical, and restrictive. While no one is homeless, hungry, or unemployed, while gold, silver, gems, and other material goods hold no greater value than their use in everyday life (gold, for example, is made into chamber pots!), while all individuals are free to meet all their needs, nevertheless they are rigidly constrained in what they are able or encouraged to do. Personal freedom is highly restricted. Individuals are not free to satisfy their desires: debating politics outside the popular assembly is a capital offense; one must get police permission to travel, and even the permission of one's father or spouse in order to take a walk in the countryside. While extolling the virtues of this idealized culture, "More," the fictional narrator of the two books comprising *Utopia* (who is surprisingly close to More, the author of *Utopia*), enigmatically ends Book 2 by dissociating himself from many of Utopia's customs and laws, claiming them absurd and ridiculous, even though he also claims that many others would be worth importing to Europe.

What is significant for our purposes here, though, is the question that intrigued so many of More's commentators: Why did More invent a recognizably flawed ideal? The other, more obvious, alternatives—an idealized representation of a perfect commonwealth, or the satire of a bad one—seem more straightforward options. Why invent a nonideal, or rather, an equivocal ideal? Why compromise and endanger the idealized dimension of the literary and imaginative project with a realism that explains the necessary conditions and consequences of the production of political ideals?

This dilemma is compressed into the very name of that ideal—Utopia. In More's neologism, the term is linguistically ambiguous, the result of two different fusions from Greek roots: the adverb *ou*—"not"—and the noun *topos*—"place": no-place. But More is also punning on another Greek composite, *eutopia*, "happy," "fortunate," or "good" place. Many commentators have suggested that this pun signals the ideal, or fictional, status of accounts of the perfect society: the happy or fortunate place, the good place, is no place—no place, that is, except in imagination. I would like to suggest a different reading of this pun: not the good place is no place, but rather no place is the good place. The utopic is beyond a conception of space or place because the utopic, ironically, cannot be regarded as topological at all. It does not conform to a logic of spatiality. It is thus conceivable, and perhaps even arguable, that the utopic is beyond the architectural (insofar as architecture is the domain for the regulation and manipulation of made spaces and places; insofar as its domain or purview has remained geographical, geological, site-specific, location-oriented—that is, insofar as its milieu is spatialized, in the sense of being localized and conceptualized only in spatial terms). Architecture remains out of touch with the fundamental movement of the utopic, the movement to perfection or to the ideal, which is adequately conceivable only in the temporal dimension, and above all in the temporal modality of the future.

What Plato, More, and virtually every other thinker of utopia share, though the picture each presents of an ideal society fluctuates and varies immensely according to political ideologies, is this: the utopic is always conceived as a *space*, usually an enclosed and isolated space—the walled city, the isolated island, a political and agrarian self-contained organization, and thus a commonwealth. The space is self-regulating, autonomous from, though it may function alongside of and in exchange with, other states and regions. The utopic is definitionally conceived in the topological mode, as a place with definite contours and features. As Margaret Whitford points out, the utopic perpetually verges on the dystopic, the dysfunctional utopia, the more modern these utopic visions become.[4] The atopic, the inverted other of the utopic and its ghostly dystopic accompaniment, is not a place, but rather a non-place (in its own way, it too is always *ou*-topic), an indeterminate place, but place and space nevertheless.[5]

This emphasis on place and space is no doubt why the utopic has been a locus of imagination and invention for architects, as well as for political theorists, activists, and fiction writers: descriptions of buildings and municipal arrangements figure quite prominently in Plato's, Aristotle's, and More's accounts of ideal political regulation. But the slippage into the dystopic may also help explain why the architectural imaginary that peoples such utopic visions almost invariably produces an architecture of direct control (architecture as that which directly or neutrally facilitates the subject's control over its political and natural environment), an architecture of political inflexibility. Until the dimension of time or duration has an impact on the ways in which architecture is theorized and practiced, the utopic, with its dual impossibility and necessity, will remain outside architectural reach and beyond its effect. The utopic is not that which can be planned and built, for that is to imply that it is already an abstract possibility that merely requires a mode or realization. It mistakes a possibility for a virtuality, a preformed structure for a dynamically and organically developing one. This failure to conceive of utopia as a mode of temporality and thus as a mode of becoming is clearly witnessed in the two large-scale "artificial" cities planned, designed, and built according to an abstract plan: Canberra and Brasília, barely representative of utopic design but both planned as communities supporting a civic and political center, and thus as cities whose architectural conception would facilitate their functioning as the seat of government. In other words, they are cities that have come as close as possible, in their realization, to the abstract and rational plan that governs philosophical utopias. Ironically, of course, both cities have long been recognized, almost since their inception, as supremely "practical" and yet largely unlivable, restricted in their capacity for organic growth and for surprise.

Can architecture construct a better future? How can it do so without access to another notion of time than that of projection and planned development (a time in which the future is fundamentally the same as the past, or increases in some formulaic version of the past)? What could a utopic architecture be, if architecture remains grounded in the spatial alone? How, in other words, is architecture, as theory and as practice, able to find its own place in politics, and, above all, its own place in the unpredictable becoming of the movement of time and duration? How can architecture, as the art or science of spatial organization, open itself up to the temporal movements that are somehow still beyond its domain?

The Future

If utopia is the good place that is no place, if utopias, by their very nature, involve the fragile negotiation between an ideal mode of social and political regulation and the cost that must be borne by the individuals thus regulated, then it is clear that they involve not only the political and social organization of space and power—which Plato and More have recognized and specifically addressed—but also two elements that remain marked, if unremarked upon, in their works: the notion of time as becoming (the utopic as a dimension of the virtual, an admixture of the latency of the past and the indeterminacy of the future, the mode of linkage between an inert past, conceived as potential, and a future not yet in existence); and a conception of the bodies that are the object of utopic, political, and temporal speculations. In short, the utopic cradles in the force field composed of several vectors: its "strange attractors" are triangulated through three processes or systems: (1) the forces and energies of bodies, bodies that require certain material, social, and cultural arrangements to function in specific or required ways, and which in turn, through their structuring and habitual modes, engender and sustain certain modes of political regulation; (2) the pull or impetus of time, which grants a precedence of the future over the past and the present, and which threatens to compromise or undo whatever fixity and guarantees of progress, whatever planning and organization we seek in the present; and (3) the regulation and organization, whether literary or phantasmatic or pragmatic, of urban and rural spaces of inhabitation.

This triangulation has been rendered less complicated by the common move of dropping out or eliding one of these three terms—usually that represented by time and becoming. It is significant that the question of the future in and of the Republic, the future of the Utopians, remains unaddressed; utopia, like the dialectic itself, is commonly fantasized as the end of time, the end of history, the moment of resolution of past problems. The utopic organization is conceived as a machine capable of solving foreseeable problems through the perfection of its present techniques. This is the image of an ideal society in which time stops and, as Plato recognized, the timeless sets it. If we explore the plethora of other utopic visions, from Francis Bacon's *New Atlantis*, to the general project of the social contract theorists in the eighteenth century, to Voltaire, Rousseau's *The New Héloïse* and *The Social Contract*, through to Hegel's *Phenomenology of Mind*, we see that the ideal society, society in its perfection, is represented as the cessation of becoming, the overcoming of problems, a calm and ongoing resolution. While a picture of the future, the utopic is fundamentally that which *has no future*, that place whose organization is so controlled that the future ceases to be the most pressing concern. These utopias function as the exercise of fantasies of control over what Foucault has called "the event," that which is unprepared for, unforeseeable, singular, unique, and transformative, the advent of something new. Indeed it is precisely against this idea of newness, creation, or advent that the fantasy of utopia, of a perfect and controlled society, is developed to reassure us.[6] Utopias can be understood as further mechanisms or procedures whose function is precisely to provide reassurances of a better future, of the necessity for planning and preparedness, and rational reflection, in the face of an unknowable future.

Whether developed in the past or developed today in science fiction and cinema, all utopic visions share the desire to freeze time, to convert the movement of time into the arrangements of space, to produce the future on the model of the (limited and usually self-serving) ideals of the present. Michèle Le Doeuff argues that this may explain why so many utopian texts are actually double texts, texts that are composites or amalgams, with a self-contained utopic, fictional account that is explained and justified through a theoretical addendum, commonly a text written after the more speculative and fanciful account. Looking at the history of utopic discourses, we can see that from the beginning the fictional seems to be coupled with the theoretical, without any adequate attempt to modify or transform the fictional or to incorporate the theoretical and justificatory elements into it. To the theoretical disposition of Plato's *Republic*, Le Doeuff counterposes his *Laws;* to Book 2 of *Utopia* must be counterposed the long analysis of private property and theft in contemporary England that comprises Book 1; to Rousseau's *Social Contract,* there is *Projet de constitution pour la Corse;* to Kepler's science-fictional *Somnium,* there is his theoretical treatise *Astronomia nova.* Le Doeuff's explanation of this awkward but prevalent coupling of theory and vision, in brief, is that the theoretical or analytical doublet is written in part to contain the ambiguity, or as she calls it, the polysemic quality, of the visionary text in an attempt to fix its meaning, to provide it a guaranteed reading:

The point is, in short, that if Utopia had consisted only in its second part, a *de facto* plurality of readings would be possible. But Book I establishes the canonical reading and privileges the political meaning of Book II at the expense of others: as Book I is *essentially* a critique of the social and political organization of England, a denunciation of private property and the English penal system, Book II is taken as being *essentially* a description of the best possible Republic. By writing Book I, More himself provides a principle for decoding his initial text.[7]

In other words, the function of theoretical doubling of the utopic texts is to contain ambiguity, to control how the text is read, to control the very future that the ideal is designed to protect or ensure. At the very moment when the impulse to project a better future takes form, the theoretical component attempts to contain what it invokes: the untidy, unsettling singularity of time, the precedence that temporal flow has over any given image or process, utopic or otherwise. Utopic models commonly require a duplicated theoretical justification because every model both establishes and paradoxically undermines its idealized vision, putting an end to political problems of the present and projecting for itself no problem-solving role in its future: utopia has no future, the future has already come as its present (which is why utopia has no place, but also, even more ironically, why it has no time: the utopic is that which is out of time).

While I do not have the time (or space) here to elaborate in much detail what such a conception of time involves, I have written elsewhere on the notion of duration, virtuality, and the architectural field.[8] What I can do here is outline some of its most salient elements:

1. Time, or more precisely, duration, is always singular, unique, and unrepeatable. Henri Bergson, the great theorist of duration, has suggested that duration is simultaneously singular and a multiplicity. Each duration forms a continuity, a single, indivisible movement; and yet, there are many simultaneous durations, implying that all durations participate in a generalized or cosmological duration, which allows them to be described as simultaneous. Duration is the very condition of simultaneity, as well as succession. An event occurs only once: it has its own characteristics, which will never occur again, even in repetition. But it occurs alongside of, simultaneous with, many other events, whose rhythms are also specific and unique. Duration is thus the milieu of qualitative difference.

2. The division of duration—which occurs whenever time is conceptualized as a line, counted, divided into before and after, made the object of the numerical, rendering its analog continuity into digital or discrete units—transforms its nature, that is to say, reduces it to modes of spatiality. If, as Bergson suggests, space is the field of quantitative differences, of differences of degree, then the counting of time, its linear representation, reduces and extinguishes its differences of kind to replace them with

differences of degree (the source of many philosophical illusions and paradoxes—most notably Zeno's paradox).

3. One of the most significant differences of kind within duration (which is commonly misunderstood as a difference of degree) is the distinction between past and present. The past and the present are not two modalities of the present, the past a receded or former present, a present that has moved out of the limelight. Rather, the past and the present fundamentally coexist; they function in simultaneity. Bergson suggests that the whole of the past is contained, in contracted form, in each moment of the present. The past is the virtuality that the present, the actual, carries along with it. The past lives *in time*. The past could never exist if it did not coexist with the present of which it is the past, and thus with every present.[9]

The past would be inaccessible to us altogether if we could gain access to it only through the present and its passing. The only access we have to the past is through a leap into virtuality, through a move into the past itself, given that, for Bergson, the past is outside us and that we are in it rather than it being located in us. The past exists, but it is in a state of latency or virtuality. We must place ourselves in it if we are to have recollections, memory images.

4. If the present is the actuality whose existence is engendered by the virtual past, then the future remains that dimension or modality of time that has no actuality either. The future too remains virtual, uncontained by the present but prefigured, rendered potential, through and by the past. The future is that over which the past and present have no control: the future is that openness of becoming that enables divergence from what exists. This means that, rather than the past exerting a deterministic force over the future (determinism reduces the future to the present!), the future is that which overwrites or restructures the virtual that is the past: the past is the condition of every fu-

ture; the future that emerges is only one of the lines of virtuality from the past. The past is the condition for infinite futures, and duration is that flow that connects the future to the past which gave it impetus.

What does this notion of time mean for the concept of the utopian and for embodied utopias? That the utopian is not the projection of a future at all, although this is how it is usually understood; rather, it is the projection of a past or present as if it were the future. The utopian is in fact a freezing of the indeterminable movement from the past through the future that the present is unable to directly control. Utopian discourses attempt to compensate for this indetermination between past and future, and for the failure of the present to represent a site of control for this movement to and of the future. The utopian mode seeks a future that itself has no future, a future in which time will cease to be a relevant factor, and movement, change, and becoming remain impossible.[10]

Bodies

How do bodies fit into the utopic? In what sense can the utopic be understood as embodied? Here, I want to suggest two contradictory movements: on the one hand, every idea of the utopic, from Plato through More to present-day utopians, conceptualizes the ideal commonwealth in terms of the management, regulation, care, and ordering of bodies. Each pictures a thoroughly embodied social organization. On the other hand, there is no space or future, in utopic visions, for the production of a position that acknowledges the sexual, racial, etc., specificity and differential values of its subjects. No utopia has been framed to take account of the diversity not only of subjects but also of their utopic visions, that is, to the way in which visions of the ideal are themselves reflections of the specific positions occupied in the present.

All philosophical utopias have dealt with the question of bodies. While they idealize the potential relations between individual and collective bodies, none of them advocates a decorporeal or disembodied state. After all, what a social organization consists in, above all, is the production, regulation and management of bodies through the production of practices, habits, rituals, and institutions. The problem is *not* that the various visions of the utopic promulgated over the last three millennia lack an interest in the corporeal. Moreover, it is significant that even the question of relations between the sexes seems to play a major role in historical representations of the ideal commonwealth.

In well-known passages of Book V of the *Republic*, for example, Plato expounds on the ideal arrangements between the sexes to ensure the maximal functioning of the polis. He argues that, just as there are individual differences distinguishing the capacities and abilities of one man from those of another, so there are individual differences among women's abilities. There is no reason why the best of women, like the best of men, should not be educated to the guardian class, and be rulers of the Republic: "With a view to having women guardians, we should not have one kind of education to fashion the men, and another for the women, especially as they have the same nature to begin with."[11] Furthermore, Plato suggests that marriage and sexual monogamy should be eliminated, and a controlled, self-constrained sexual and child-raising collective should be instituted in their place: "All these women shall be wives in common to all the men, and not one of them shall live privately with any man; the children too should be held in common so that no parent shall know which is his offspring, and no child shall know his parent."[12]

This same concern for the status of sexual relations and the place of women and children preoccupies a good part of the work of More. Because women work equally alongside men, there is prosperity. Because twice as many people work in Utopia as in Europe, the work day is only six hours long. On the other hand, the rules governing marriage, divorce, and sexual relations are strict to produce a narrow, lifelong, and nondeceptive monogamy. More explains that the Utopian marital customs may strike Europeans as strange, but they are more direct and honest:

In choosing marriage partners they solemnly and seriously follow a custom which seemed to us foolish and absurd in the extreme. Whether she be a widow or virgin, the bride-to-be is shown naked to the groom by a responsible and respectable matron; and similarly, some respectable man presents the groom naked to his prospective bride. We laughed at this custom, and called it absurd; but they were just as amazed at the folly of all other people. When they go to buy a colt, where they are risking only a little money, they are so cautious that, though the animal is almost bare, they won't close the deal until the saddle and blanket have been taken off, lest there be a hidden sore underneath. Yet in the choice of a mate, which may cause either delight or disgust for the rest of their lives, men are so careless that they leave the rest of the woman's body covered up with clothes. . . .

There is extra reason for them to be careful, because in that part of the world they are the only people who practice monogamy, and because their marriages are seldom terminated except by death—though they do allow divorce for adultery or for intolerable offensive behavior.[13]

All the major writers on utopias devote considerable detail in their texts to various arrangements, some apparently egalitarian, others clearly hierarchized, regarding marital rights and duties and the sexual and social responsibilities and rights of men, women, and children. All make an underlying assumption of the fundamental unity and singularity, the neutrality and quasi-universality of the state (excluding slaves/bondsmen). The commonwealth, though it may differentiate men and women in their roles, nevertheless equalizes them in the protection it appears to offer for their socially validated positions. So, although the question of embodiment is discussed in considerable detail in terms of the relations between the sexes and the adjudication of their proper roles, the question of sexual difference has not been adequately raised. Instead of this question, the question of women's place within an apparently neutral but visibly patriarchal and fraternal social order takes its place—the question of accommodating women within frameworks that have been devised according to what men think is sexually neutral. This may explain the apparent strangeness of More's decree regarding the right of betrothed couples to view each other naked before marriage, as a man would view a horse he was purchasing! Egalitarianism consists in extending to women, or to other cultural minorities, the rights accorded to the dominant group; it does *not* consist in rethinking the very nature of those rights in relation to those groups whom it was originally designed to exclude or constrain. Plato extends to women the same rights he has already deduced for men. The same is true, and even more visibly, in More's text: women remain the same as men insofar as the law, the economy, and the judiciary require it; yet they remain men's complements where it suits men![14]

In Irigaray's terminology, relations between the sexes have only ever been subjected to a relation of sexual *indifference*, there has been no conceptualization of a *dual sexual symmetry*—in other words, any understanding that perhaps women's conceptions of the universal good may differ from men's has yet to be adequately articulated.[15]

Irigaray's claim, which in many ways is relevant to the theme of embodied utopias, is that sexual difference is that which has yet to take place; it is that which has staked a place in the future. Sexual difference does not yet exist, and it is possible that it has never existed. In the history of the West, since at least the time of Plato, the ideals of culture, knowledge, and civilization have practiced a resolute sexual *indifference*, in which the interests of women were seen as parallel or complementary to those of men. The sexes as we know them today, and even the sexes as posed in many feminist visions of a postpatriarchal utopia, have only one model, a singular and universal neutrality. At best, equal participation is formulated. But the idea of sexual difference, which entails the existence of *at least two* points of view, sets of interests, perspectives, two types of ideal, two modes of knowledge, has yet to be considered. It is, in a sense, beyond the utopian, for the utopian has always been the present's projection of a singular and universal ideal, the projection of the present's failure to see its own modes of neutralization. Sexual difference, like the utopic, is a category of the future anterior, Irigaray's preferred tense for writing, the only tense that openly addresses the question of the future without, like the utopian vision, preempting it. Which is not to say, as I have already intimated, that sexual difference is a utopian ideal.[16]

On the contrary, because sexual difference is one of the present's ways of conceptualizing its current problems, all the work of sexual difference, its labor of producing alternative knowledges, methods, and criteria, has yet to begin. It is beyond the utopian insofar as no vision, narrative, or plan of the ideal society, or idealized relations between the sexes, can perform this work of *making difference:* it is entirely of the order of the surprise, the encounter with the new. Irigaray saves herself from the tiresome charges of essentialism and utopianism by refusing to speculate on what this sexual difference might consist of or how it might manifest itself. She sees that the future for feminism is that which is to be made rather than foreseen or predicted: "To concern oneself in the present about the future certainly does not consist in programming it in advance but in trying to bring it into existence."[17]

How, then, can we understand the idea of embodied utopias? What would utopias that consider embodiment be like? And how might they be relevant to the concerns of architecture? Here I have only some suggestions:

1. Architecture itself should not be so much concerned with seeking to build, perform, or enact ideals or ideal solutions to contemporary or future problems; indeed, it is a goal-directedness that utopic visions orient us toward, in neglecting the notion of process, precisely because they do not understand the role of time. The solution to the political and social problems of the present, while clearly a good thing for architects to keep in mind in their labors of planning and building, should not be the goal or purpose of either architecture or politics. Rather, the radical role of the architect is best developed in architectural exploration and invention, in the recognition of the ongoing need for exploration and invention, in recognition of the roles of architecture and knowledge as experimental practices. Philosophy, architecture, and science are not disciplines that produce answers or solutions but fields that pose questions, whose questions never yield the solutions they seek but which lead to the production of ever more inventive questions. Architecture, along with life itself, moves alongside of—is the ongoing process of negotiating—habitable spaces. Architecture is a set of highly provisional "solutions" to the question of how to live and inhabit space with others. It is a negotiation with one of the problems life poses to bodies, a spatial question-raising that subjects itself, as all questions and solutions do, to the movements of time and becoming.

2. Too much of politics is devoted to the question of blueprints, plans, preparation for the unexpected. Although it is one of the functions of architecture to devise plans, to make blueprints, to prepare in every detail for the future building it is anticipating, this precision and determinacy of planning must not be confused with the kinds of planning that are required for political organization and reorganization, where, as concrete as they may be in conception, they always prove to be indeterminable in their application. An adequate acknowledgment of the vicissitudes of futurity would ensure that we abandon the fantasy of controlling the future while not abdicating the responsibility of preparing for a better future than the present.

3. For architecture to have a future in which embodiment plays a self-conscious and positive role, it is crucial that sexual difference have its effects there, as well as in other spheres of life. This suggestion is not to be confused with the call for "gender parity" in the profession. Rather, as the field of architecture undergoes self-examination and self-reflection, its practitioners and theorists must acknowledge that the history of architecture is only one among many possible histories, and acknowledge the debt that the dominant discourses and practices of architecture owe to the practices and discourses that were either discarded or ignored, or never invented or explored. This is the role that embodiment plays in the history of architecture—the labor of architectural invention, the collective efforts of millennia of architects, builders, engineers, including those whose efforts are not preserved by history and those who were actively excluded from participation. Architecture as a discipline is always already a mode of embodiment *and* a mode of the disavowal of a debt to embodiment. This is, for want of a better phase, the critique

of its own phallocentrism that architecture must undertake. Such a critique is not to be mistaken for the charges of gender imbalance, which are certainly relevant, but correcting the imbalance is not enough. Architecture, like all other disciplines, needs to come to grips with its own *phallocentrism*, which is to say, its own structures of disavowed debt and obligation, to a recognition that its "identity," as fluctuating and fragile as it might be, is contingent upon that which it "others" or excludes. This other is its "feminine," the virtualities not actualized in the present, the impetus for the future anterior.

4. The relation between bodies, social structures, and built living and work environments and their ideal interactions is not a question that can be settled: the very acknowledgment of the multiplicity of bodies and their varying political interests and ideals implies that there are a multiplicity of idealized solutions to living arrangements, arrangements about collective coexistence, but it is no longer clear that a single set of relations, a single goal or ideal, will ever adequately serve as the neutral ground for any consensual utopic form. Utopias are precisely not about consensus but about the enactment of ideals of the privileged, ideals of the government by the few of the many, ideals not derived from consensus but designed to produce or enforce it. In short, ideals need to be produced over and over again, and their proliferation and multiplication is an ongoing process, always a measure of dissatisfaction with the past and present, always the representation of ever-receding futures. The task for architecture, as for philosophy, is not to settle on utopias, models, concrete ideals, but instead to embark on the process of endless questioning.

The transition to a new age requires a change in our perception and conception of space-time, the inhabiting of places, and of containers, or envelopes of identity. It assumes and entails an evolution or a transformation of forms, of the relations of matter and form and of the interval between: the trilogy of the constitution of place.

Luce Irigaray, *An Ethics of Sexual Difference*

1. Spatial Excess

I am concerned in this chapter with the ways in which architecture and conceptions of space and habitation always contain within themselves an excess, an extra dimension, that takes them above and beyond the concerns of mere functionality, their relevance for the present, and into the realm of the future where they may function differently. To understand the excessiveness, the abundance and potential for proliferation in architecture, one might address not only the ways in which it addresses social and community needs, but also the ways in which it leaves unaddressed that which is left out of social collectives, which glues collectives together while finding its existence only outside, as marginalized. There is a community, a collective of those who have nothing in common. This concept of a community of the lost, of strangers, of the marginalized and outcast is borrowed from the work of Alphonso Lingis, and especially from his concern with community not as that which is united through common bonds, goals, language, or descent, but as that which opens itself to the stranger, to the dying, to the one with whom one has nothing in common, the one who is not like oneself. Lingis is concerned with the community that is possible only with an alien, that is, an otherness that cannot be absorbed into commonness:

> Community forms when one exposes oneself to the naked one, the destitute one, the outcast, the dying one. One enters into community not by affirming oneself and one's forces but by exposing oneself to expenditure at a loss, to sacrifice. Community forms in a movement by which one exposes oneself to the other, to forces and powers outside oneself, to death and to the others who die.[1]

Communities, which make language, culture, and thus architecture their modes of existence and expression, come into being not through the recognition, generation, or establishment of common interests, values, and needs, and the establishment of universal, neutral laws and conventions that bind and enforce them (as social contractarians proclaim), but through the remainders they cast out, the figures they reject, the terms that they consider unassimilable, that they attempt to sacrifice, revile, and expel.[2] There are many names for this unassimilable residue: the other, the abject, the scapegoat, the marginalized, the destitute, the refugee, the dying, etc. I will call this residue "more" or "excess," but this "more" is not simply superadded but also undermines and problematizes.

Excess is a concept that itself has a long and illustrious philosophical history, being the object of reflection from at least the time of Aristotle—the great theorist of moderation, to whom I will return. However, the greatest theorists of excess arguably must be understood in the lineage of philosophers that follows in the tradition from Nietzsche: most especially the tradition of French Nietzscheans—Marcel Mauss, Georges Bataille, Pierre Klossowski, René Girard, Jacques Derrida, Gilles Deleuze, Julia Kristeva, Luce Irigaray. This conception of excess as that which outstrips and finds no stable place in orderly systems, or within systematicity itself, as that whose very systematicity defies the laws of system, can be identified, on the one hand, through the dramatizations of Bataille, of the excess as the order of the excremental; and on the other, in the writings of Irigaray, where this excess is cast as the maternal-feminine.

For Bataille, dirt, disorder, contagion, expenditure, filth, immoderation—and above all, shit—exceed the proper, what constitutes "good taste," good form, measured production. If the world of the proper, the system, form, regulated production, constitutes an economy—a restricted economy—a world of exchange, use, and expedience, then there is an excess, a remainder, an uncontained element, the "accursed share"—a "general economy"—a world or order governed by immoderation, excess, and sacrifice, an economy of excremental proliferations, which expresses itself most ably in "unproductive expenditure: luxury, mourning, war, cults, the construction of sumptuary monuments, games, spectacles, arts, perverse sexual activity."[3] Bataille posits one economy of production and consumption that constitutes an ordered and measured system of circulation, and another economy preoccupied with conspicuous and disproportionate expenditure, with consumption and a logic of crippling obligation. This distinction runs through not only social, cultural, and economic relations; significantly, it also underlies a distinction between types of art, and within particular forms of art, the arts or crafts of use and reference, and those of proliferation, the superficial, and the ornamental.

On the one hand, Bataille claims that architecture itself may function as a measured, calculated economy. Indeed, in his earlier writings, he develops a rather banal, quasi-psychoanalytic understanding of the skyscraper and of architectural functioning as phallic symbol in an aggressive access to the feminine sky it "scrapes."[4] As he first defines it, architecture is that which places man midway between the monkey and the machine: "Man would seem to represent merely an intermediary stage within the morphological development between monkey and building."[5] Architecture represents an intermediary between the animal and the mechanical, retaining some of the traces of its inhuman, animal origin, as well as the anticipation or movement toward the fully mechanized, the reign of authoritarian control. In this sense, architecture, as Bataille describes it, represents not the physiognomy of the people, or of culture as a whole, but of its bureaucratic and petty officials; and the spirit of excess is perhaps best represented in the *destruction* of monumental architecture rather than in any positive architectural production:

In fact, only society's ideal nature—that of authoritative command and prohibition—expresses itself in actual architectural constructions. Thus great monuments rise up like dams, opposing a logic of majesty and authority to all unquiet elements. . . . Indeed, monuments obviously inspire good social behaviour and often even genuine fear. The fall of the Bastille is symbolic of this state of things. This mass movement is difficult to explain otherwise than by popular hostility towards monuments which are their veritable masters.[6]

If rage and destruction—the fall of the Bastille—are the provocative response of the masses to the increasing functionality and bureaucratization of interwar architecture, Bataille suggests that perhaps a return to expenditure, to the animal, to the excessive and the redundant, to tread a path already explored in painting (one imagines here a reference to Dada and surrealism) in the architectural may pose an alternative model: "However strange this may seem when a creature as elegant as the human being is involved, a path—traced by the painters—opens up toward bestial monstrosity, as if there were no other way of escaping the architectural straitjacket."[7]

As Bataille identifies it, architecture must seek its own excesses, its bestial monstrosity, its allegiances with forces, affects, energies, experiments, rather than with ordinances, rules, function, or form. We must ask, following this understanding of the place of the excessive as transgression, how to engender an architectural "bestial monstrosity," a radically antifunctional architecture, an architecture that is anti-authoritarian and antibureaucratic. An architecture that refuses to function in and be part of, as Deleuze names them, "societies of control." This is perhaps a more powerful provocation today than when Bataille first raised it. It may bring about a "politics of the impossible," the only kind of politics, as Lingis recognized, worth struggling for. For Bataille, what is "more" or "excessive" is that which has no function, purpose, or other use than the expenditure of resources and energy, is that which undermines, transgresses, and countermands the logic of functionality. The ornament, the detail, the redundant, and the unnecessary: these may prove provisional elements of any architectures of excess (instead of the Bastille, Winchester House?).

2. Spatialized Femininity

If Bataille is perhaps the best representation of the excremental pole of the beam of excess, then it could be argued that the other pole, its counterbalance, is the feminine or femininity. The excremental and the excessive cannot simply be identified with the repressed or unconscious elements of oneself and one's collective identifications (indeed, it is only a certain concept of a pure and clean masculinity that renders the anal, rather than the feminine, as its other). Its most crucial condition is its otherness, its outsideness to the systems that it exceeds and outstrips. Whereas cultural excess is, on the one hand, represented (in Bataille) in the animal, the bestial, the bodily, and especially in bodily waste, it is also represented (in the work of Irigaray and other feminist theorists) by that which is othered, rendered as a kind of human representation of this waste, Woman and femininity. Bataille himself makes clear the associations and connections between the excremental, the fluid, and femininity.[8] But it is not clear that we can accept or share in Bataille's vision, derived as it is from psychoanalysis, of femininity as wound, blood, loss, and castration. Instead, we may see the place of femininity as that which the architectural cannot contain within its own drives to orderliness and systematicity, its own specifically architectural excesses. For this concept, Irigaray's work may prove immensely suggestive, even if, like Bataille, Lingis, Deleuze, and others, she actually has written very little that is directed specifically to the question of architecture. Architectural practitioners must undertake this labor for themselves—a specifically architectural understanding of excess, of more, of that which exceeds the architectural.

Irigaray's work, like that of the others, is directed more to philosophical concepts of space, place, and dwelling than to architectural, social, or communitarian projects. Nevertheless, like Bataille's, her philosophical positions regarding the excessive, innumerable, and unmappable territories that make the very notion of territory, possession, and self-containment possible remind us clearly that any notion of order, system, community, knowledge, and control—especially those involved in the architectural project (from conception through to planning, building, and inhabitation)—entails a notion of excess, expenditure, and loss that can be closely associated with those elements of femininity and of woman that serve to distinguish women as irreducible to and not exhausted in the masculine and the patriarchal. Irigaray's consistent claim is that the question of difference—which is lived most vividly and irreducibly, though not only, in sexual difference—requires a rethinking of the relations between space and time: "In order to make it possible to think through, and live, this difference, we must reconsider the whole problematic of *space* and *time*."[9]

Such a reconsideration would involve at least three major factors: (1) a reconceptualization of space and time as oppositional forms (one the mode of simultaneity, the other the mode of succession); (2) a reconceptualization of the ways in which the space/time opposition has been historically and conceptually associated with the opposition between femininity and masculinity, that is, the ways in which femininity is spatialized, rendered substance or medium to the interiority and duration attributed to the (masculinized) subject of duration;[10] and (3) a reconceptualization of the modes of inhabitation that each has and makes on the other, a concept that Irigaray defines as the interval, the envelope, the passage in between, but which we could also describe as the excess or remainder, the "more" left over between them. The interval, undecidably spatial and temporal, insinuates a temporal delay in all spatial presence, and a spatial extension of all temporal intensity; it is the site of their difference and their interchange, the movement or passage from one existence to another. The inscription of a different kind of space may provide the possibility of exchange between and across difference, space, or spaces, may become a mode of accommodation and inhabitation rather than a commonness that communities divide and share. Irigaray claims that until the feminine can be attributed an interiority of its own, a subjectivity, and thus a duration, while it continues to provide the resources for masculinized subjectivity and time by providing them with space, it has no space of its own and no time of its own. It is not that Irigaray is seeking a space/place or time for women alone. Quite the contrary, she is seeking modes of conceptualizing and representing space—preconditions to occupying and using it differently—that are more in accordance with the kinds of space, and time, repressed or unrepresented in the conventional structure of opposition between them.

If sexual difference requires a reordering of space and time, then what must be reordered? Irigaray suggests that the surreptitious association of femininity with spatiality has had two discernible if unarticulated effects. First, woman is rendered the enigmatic ground, substance, or material undifferentiation, the place of origin of both subjectivity and objectivity, that is, of masculinity and the objects in which it finds itself reflected. Femininity becomes the space, or better, *the matrix*, of male self-unfolding. Second, the feminine becomes elaborated as darkness and abyss, as void and chaos, as that which is both fundamentally spatial and as that which deranges or unhinges the smooth mapping and representation of space, a space that is too self-proximate, too self-enclosed to provide the neutrality, the coordinates, of self-distancing, to produce and sustain a homogeneous, abstract space. The feminine becomes a matrix that defies coordinates, that defies the systematic functioning of matrices that propose to order and organize the field.

Irigaray argues that the very constitution of the field of space-time—with space as the field of external and extended positions and connections, and time as the field of internal and subjective positions and connections—is already set up in such a way that space is defined as smooth, continuous, homogeneous, passive, and neutral, as that which has no folds, no complexity, no interior or intensity of its own. It is already set up such that it morphologically reproduces the passive attributes of femininity. Irigaray maintains that woman has represented place for man, and more than that, the kind of place she has provided is a specific one: she functions as container, as envelope, as that which surrounds and marks the limit of man's identity. This is a paradoxical relation: woman comes to provide the place in which and through which man can situate himself as subject, which means that she represents a place that has no place, that has no place of its own but functions only as place for another.[11]

The maternal-feminine remains the *place separated from "its" own place*, deprived of "its" place. She is or ceaselessly becomes the place of the other who cannot separate himself from it. With her knowing or willing it, she is then threatened because of what she lacks: a "proper" place. She would have to re-envelop herself with herself, and do so at least twice: as a woman and as a mother. Which would presuppose a change in the whole economy of space-time.[12]

Irigaray discusses a perverse exchange at the origin of space, and thus, as the archaic precondition of architecture itself: in exchange for the abstract space of scientific and technological manipulation that man extracts from the maternal-feminine body from which he comes, he gives woman a container or envelope that he has taken from her to form his own identity, and to ensure that she continues to look after and sustain it. The container: the home, clothes, jewels, things he constructs for her, or at least for the image of her, that allow him to continue his spatial appropriations with no sense of obligation, debt, or otherness. The exchange: she gives him a world; he confines her in his:

Again and again, taking from the feminine the tissue or texture of spatiality. In exchange—but it isn't a real one—he buys her a house, even shuts her up in it, places limits, unwittingly situates her. He contains or envelops her with walls while enveloping himself and his things with her flesh. The nature of these envelopes is not the same: on the one hand, invisibly alive, but with barely perceivable limits; on the other, visibly limiting or sheltering, but at the risk of being prison-like or murderous if the threshold is not left open.[13]

The maternal-feminine (indeed, the feminine as wrapped up in the very space, commonly described as "confinement," of the maternal, and so a space that is always doubled up on itself, self-enfolded in itself) becomes the invisible, spaceless ground of space and visibility, the "mute substratum" that opens up the world as that which can be measured, contained, and conquered. In Irigaray's conception, the attribution of a more or less porous membrane to the feminine, the refusal to grant it its own interior, means that the space of the inside becomes the ground or terrain for the exploitation of the exterior: "Don't we always put ourselves inside out for this architecture?"[14] she asks, which is why it is so hard to find one's place there: space itself is erected on that very place covered over by construction and thus rendered impossible for habitation!

Lost in your labyrinth, you look for me without even realizing that this maze is built from my flesh. You have put me inside out and you look for me in retroversion where you can't find me. You are lost in me, far from me. You have forgotten that I also have an interior . . .[15]

The conceptual turning inside-out of the maternal-feminine, as if it had no interiority and thus no time of its own, facilitated the cultural universe that replaces it and enables that universe to expand and present itself as space, as spatiality, as that which is to be inhabited, colonized, made of use, invested with value—as that which can be calculated, measured, rendered mappable through coordinates, made into a matrix, the space of temporal planning. But this maneuver is not without its own ironic costs: in taking the world, nature, the bodies of others, as the ground or material of speculation (in both its economic and conceptual senses), man as explorer, scientist, or architect has lost the resources of his own specificity (those limited resources provided by his own corporeality), as well as those which nurtured and grounded him.

Bataille is right to suggest that monumental and memorial architectures are the architectures of totalitarianism, the architecture of societies of control, of phallic consumption; his work clearly anticipates Irigaray's understanding of architectural and other constructions functioning as a restricted, phallic economy that overcodes and territorializes the more general economy of sexual difference and exchange, an economy of containment that envelops an economy of expenditure, or, in Derridean terms, an economy of gift. Following the logic established by Aristotelian physics, place is reduced to container, to the envelope of being; one being becomes the receptacle of another, the building or housing for another (in a sense, being becomes *fetalized*, and place, *maternalized*).[16] It is this logic that makes *place* a concept that is always already *architectural* in that it is conceived as container, limit, locus, and foundation. But this origin, and the historical fidelity of philosophical and architectural discourses to it, marks Western conceptions of place, space, and measurement with the irremovable traces of that whose being becomes backgrounded as neutral space to be taken up, given form and matter, by objects, identities, substances. Irigaray asserts that the characteristics and attributes of the maternal-feminine in Western culture—passive, neutral, fluid, formless, lacking, empty or void; a receptacle requiring filling, containment, measure—are precisely those also attributed to space, not because woman in any way resembles space, but rather because the treatment of the maternal-feminine is the condition for and template of the ways in which space is conceptualized and contained:

A certain representation of feminine jouissance corresponds to this water flowing without a container. A doubling, sought after by man, of a female *placedness*. She is assigned to be place without occupying a place. Through her, place would be set up for man's use but not hers. Her jouissance is meant to "resemble" the flow of whatever is in the place that she is when she contains, contains herself.[17]

3. Monstrous Architecture

The concept of excess, or more, enables the question of the superabundant—that which is excluded or contained because of its superabundance—to be raised as a political, as much as an economic and an aesthetic, concept. This excess, that which the sovereign, clean, proper, functional, and self-identical subject has expelled from itself, provides the conditions of all that both constitutes and undermines system, order, exchange, and production. What preconditions and overflows that thin membrane separating the outcast from the community, the container from the contained, the inside from the outside, is the embeddedness of the improper in the proper, the restricted within the general economy, the masculine within the feminine body, architecture within the body of space itself.

What, then, might provide a remedy for this constriction of space into manipulable object/neutral medium, which aligns itself with the erasure of the maternal-feminine and/or the excremental? Are there any architectural implications to be drawn from Irigaray's and Bataille's reflections on the role of those who constitute a noncommunity, a community of those who do not belong to a community? Is it possible to actively strive to produce an architecture of excess, in which the "more" is not cast off but made central, in which expenditure is sought out, in which instability, fluidity, the return of space to the bodies whose morphologies it upholds and conforms, in which the monstrous and the extrafunctional, consumption as much as production, act as powerful forces? Is this the same as or linked to the question of the feminine of architecture?

Here I will make some broad suggestions, possibly wild—even excessive—speculations:

1. If space and Aristotelian place emerge from the surreptitious neutralization and rendering passive of the maternal-feminine, then the solution to this unacknowledgeable debt is not the creation of women's spaces (or queer spaces, or the spaces of subordinated or excluded identities)—these create mere social islands within a sea of the same—but rather the exploration (scientific, artistic, architectural, and cultural) of space in different terms. When space is seen as grounded in a spatial complexity, a necessarily doubled-up and self-enfolded space providing the ground for the smooth, flat space of everyday existence, space is being defined primarily by its modes of occupation, by what occurs within it, by the mobility and growth of the objects deposited there. This notion of space as passive receptacle or nest requires either to be doubled over again—so that the nest is itself further nested without being displaced from spatial location altogether—or, more provocatively and with considerably more difficulty, space itself needs to be reconsidered in

terms of multiplicity, heterogeneity, activity, and force. Space is not simply an ether, a medium through which other forces, like gravity, produce their effects: it is inscribed by and in its turn inscribes those objects and activities placed within it.

2. Transformations in concepts of space are fundamentally linked to transformations in the concept of time. While they are considered a singular unified framework—a space-time field—and while they are understood in terms of binary oppositions, each providing what the other lacks, they remain intertwined as active and passive counterparts (in some discourses, particularly in the natural sciences, time is rendered the passive counterpart of an active space; in other discourses, particularly in the humanities, time in the form of history is the active force that ranges over passive geographical and social spaces, effecting transformation), and they inadvertently reproduce the structural relations between masculine and feminine. Space and time have their own active and passive modalities, their modes of intensity and of extension: they must be considered neither complements nor opposites but specificities, each with its own multiple modalities.

3. Architectural discourse and practice must not forget its (prehistoric or archaeological) connections to the impulse to shelter and covering first provided by nothing but the mother's body. The very concept of dwelling is irresolvably bound up with the first dwelling, itself a space enclosed within another space, and its materials—wood, metal, concrete, glass—are residues or aftereffects of the placental and bodily membranes. Rather than return to more primitive materials or openly avow these primitive maternal connections, establishing a parallel between the placental universe and the social space in which housing provides shelter (a parallel, much beloved in political philosophy, that inevitably leads to the cultural and social

space taking over the placental and natural space), architects may well find something else of value in this maternal
origin: something of immense expenditure, an economy
of pure gift, of excessive generosity, which, even if it cannot be repaid, architects could perhaps produce elsewhere,
in design and construction.

4. This idea of gift is fundamentally linked to the notion of the monstrous and the excessive (those which are
given "too much"), which defies the functionalism, the
minimalism, the drive to economy and simplicity in much
of contemporary architecture. I don't want to elevate the
idea of ornament for ornament's sake, or the idea of a
merely decorative architecture, or any particular element
within current or past architectural practice as somehow
an inherently feminine or feminist practice; I simply want
to argue that the gift of architecture is always in excess of
function, practicality, mere housing or shelter. It is also always about the celebration of an above-subsistence sociality, a cultural excess that needs elevation, not diminution.
(Indeed, the very idea of functionality is itself another
product of the cultural luxury of reflection that surpasses
need.)

5. To produce an architecture in which "women can
live" (to use Irigaray's formulation) is to produce *both* a do-
mestic and a civic architecture as envelope, which permits
the passage from one space and position to another, rather
than the containment of objects and functions in which
each thing finds its rightful place. Building would not
function as finished object but rather as spatial process,
open to whatever use it may be put to in an indeterminate
future, not as a container of solids but as a facilitator of
flows: "volume without contour," as Irigaray describes it in
Speculum.

6. And finally, an architecture of excess must aim not
to satisfy present needs but to produce future desires, not

simply to cater to pragmatic consumption but to achieve that future consummation that transforms all present intentions and purposes. Architecture is not simply the colonization or territorialization of space, though it has commonly functioned in this way, as Bataille intuited; it is also, at its best, the anticipation and welcoming of a future in which the present can no longer recognize itself. In this sense, architecture may provide some of the necessary conditions for experiments in future living, experiments in which those excluded, marginalized, and rendered outside or placeless will also find themselves.

Philosophy should be an effort to go beyond the human state.

Henri Bergson,
*The Creative Mind:
An Introduction to Metaphysics*

Things

The thing goes by many names. Indeed the very label, "the thing," is only a recent incarnation of a series of terms which have an illustrious philosophical history: the object, matter, substance, the world, noumena, reality, appearance, and so on. In the period of the Enlightenment, from Descartes to Kant, the thing became that against which we measured ourselves and our limits, the mirror of what we are not. While rare, anomalous readings of the thing emerge in post-Kantian philosophy, it is primarily associated with inert materiality. Much more recently, since the cold war, it has been associated, through this alienation from the subject, with an animated and potentially malevolent materiality, a biological materiality that is or may be the result of our unknowing (usually atomic or nuclear) intervention into nature, the revenge of the blob, of protoplasm, of radiated existence, which imperils man. Nevertheless, through these various permutations, the thing remains identified with immanence, with what we are capable of overcoming, albeit with the input of a technological supersession of the body and its reemergence in virtual form.[1] But instead of outlining *this* history, paying homage to the great thinkers of the thing, and particularly to the scientists who devoted their intellectual labors to unraveling its properties and deciphering the laws regulating its relations (the thing has become the property of the intellect and of science), I am seeking an altogether different lineage, one in which the thing is not conceived as the other, or binary double, of the subject, the self, embodiment, or consciousness, but as its condition and the resource for the subject's being and enduring. Instead of turning to Descartes or his hero, Newton, to understand things and the laws governing them, we must instead begin with Darwin and his understanding of the thing—the dynamism of the active world of natural selection—as that which provides the obstacle, the question, the means, by which life itself grows, develops, undergoes evolution and change, becomes other than what it once was. The thing is the provocation of the nonliving, the half-living, or that which has no life, to the living, to the potential of and for life.

The thing in itself is not, as Kant suggested, noumenal, that which lies behind appearances and which can never appear as such, that which we cannot know or perceive. Rather, if we follow Darwin, the thing is the real that we both find and make. The thing has a history: it is not simply a passive inertia against which we measure our own activity. It has a "life" of its own, characteristics of its own, which we must incorporate into our activities in order to be effective, rather than simply understand, regulate, and neutralize from the outside. We need to accommodate things more than they accommodate us. Life is the growing accommodation of matter, the adaptation of the needs of life to the exigencies of matter. It is matter, the thing, that produces life; it is matter, the thing, which sustains and provides life with its biological organization and orientation; and it is matter, the thing, that requires life to overcome itself, to evolve, to become more. We find the thing in the world as our resource for making things, and in the process, for leaving our trace on things. The thing is the resource for both subjects and technology.

This Darwinian inauguration of the active thing marks the beginning of a checkered, even mongrel, philosophical history, a history that culminates in a self-consciously evolutionary orientation: the inauguration of philosophical pragmatism that meanders from Darwin, through Nietzsche, to the work of Charles Sanders Peirce, William James, Henri Bergson, and eventually, through various lines of descent, into the diverging positions of Richard Rorty, on the one hand, and Gilles Deleuze on the other. These are all, in their disparate ways, pragmatist philosophers who put the questions of action, practice, and movement at the center of ontology. What these disparate thinkers share in common is little else but an understanding of the *thing as question*, as provocation, incitement, or enigma.[2] The thing, matter already configured, generates invention, the assessment of means and ends, and thus enables practice. The thing poses questions to us, questions about our needs and desires, questions above all of action: the thing is our provocation to action and is itself the result of our action. But more significantly, while the thing functions as fundamental provocation—as that which, in the virtuality of the past and the immediacy of the present cannot be ignored—it also functions as a *promise*, as that which, in the future, in retrospect, yields a destination or effect, another thing. The thing is the precondition of the living and the human, their means of survival, and the consequence or product of life and its practical needs. The thing is the point of intersection of space and time, the locus of the temporal narrowing and spatial localization that constitutes specificity or singularity.

Space and Time

The thing is born in time as well as space. It inscribes a specific duration and concrete boundaries within the broad outlines of temporal succession or flow and spatial mapping. It emerges out of and as substance. It is the coming-into-existence of a prior substance or thing, in a new time, producing beneath its processes of production a new space and a coherent entity. The thing and the space it inscribes and produces are inaugurated at the same moment, the moment that movement is arrested, frozen, or dissected to reveal its momentary aspects, the moment that the thing and the space that surrounds it are differentiated conceptually or perceptually. The moment that movement must be reflected upon or analyzed, it yields objects and their states, distinct, localized, mappable, repeatable in principle, objects and states that become the object of measurement and containment. The depositing of movement, its divisibility, and its capacity to be seen statically are the mutual conditions of the thing and of space. The thing is positioned or located in space only because time is implicated, only because the thing is the dramatic slowing down of the movements, the atomic and molecular vibrations, that frame, contextualize, and merge with and as the thing.

The thing is the transmutation, the conversion of two into one: the conversion of the previous thing, plus the energy invested in the process of its production as a different thing, a unity or a one. The making of the thing, the thing in the process of its production as a thing, is that immeasurable process that the thing must belie and disavow to be a thing. Both James and Bergson agree that, in a certain sense, although the world exists independent of us—although there is a real that remains even when the human disappears—things as such do not exist in the real. The thing is a certain carving out of the real, the (artificial or arbitrary) division of the real into entities, bounded and contained systems, that in fact only exist as open systems within the real. James provides one of the classical pragmatic descriptions of the thing:

What shall we call a *thing* anyhow? It seems quite arbitrary, for we carve out everything, just as we carve out constellations, to suit our human purposes. . . . The permanently real things for you [James's live audience] are your individual persons. To an anatomist, again, those persons are but organisms, and the real things are the organs. Not the organs, so much as their constituent cells, say the histologists; not the cells, but their molecules, say in turn, the chemists. . . . We break the flux of sensible reality into things, then, at our will.[3]

The thing is what we make of the world rather than simply what we find in the world, the way we are able to manage and regulate it according to our needs and purposes (even if not, as James suggests above, at will or consciously. We cannot but perceive the world in terms of objects. We do not do so as a matter of will). The thing is an outlined imposition we make on specific regions of the world so that these regions become comprehensible and facilitate our purposes and projects, even while limiting and localizing them. Things are our way of dealing with a world in which we are enmeshed rather than over which we have dominion. The thing is the compromise between the world as it is in its teeming and interminable multiplicity—a flux as James calls it, a continuum in Lacan's terms, or waves of interpenetrating vibrations in Bergson's understanding— and the world as we need it to be or would like it to be: open, amenable to intention and purpose, flexible, pliable, manipulable, passive. It is a compromise between mind and matter, the point of their crossing one into the other. It is our way of dealing with the plethora of sensations, vibrations, movements, and intensities that constitute both our world and ourselves, a practical exigency, indeed perhaps only one mode, not a necessary condition, of our acting in the world. James claims that we have the choice of seeing the world as objects: however, we do not. Just as Kant imposed space and time as a priori intuitions, which we have no choice but to invoke and utilize, so too we must regard objects, distinguished from other objects and from a background, as necessary, if limited, conditions under which we act in the world. Space, time, and things are conceptually connected: space and time are understood to frame and contextualize the thing; they serve as its background:

Cosmic space and cosmic time, so far from being the intuitions that Kant said they were, are constructions as patently artificial as any that science can show. The great majority of the human race never use these notions, but live in the plural times and spaces, interpenetrant and *durcheinander*.

Permanent "things" again: the "same" thing and its various "appearances" and "alterations"; the different "kinds" of things; with the "kind" used finally as a "predicate" of which the thing remains the "subject"—what a straightening of the tangle of our experience's immediate flux and sensible variety does this list of terms suggest![4]

Bergson elaborates on James's position: the world as it is in its swarming complexity cannot be an object of intelligence, for it is the function of intelligence to facilitate action and practice. The possibility of action requires that objects and their relations remain as simplified as possible, as coagulated, unified, and massive as they can be so that their contours or outlines, their surfaces, most readily promote indeterminate action. We cannot but reduce this multiplicity to the order of things and states if we are to act upon and with them, and if we are to live among things and use them for our purposes. Our intellectual and perceptual faculties function most ably when dealing with solids, with states, with things, though we find ourselves at home most readily, unconsciously or intuitively, with processes and movements:

Reality is mobile. There do not exist *things* made, but only things in the making, not *states* that remain fixed, but only states in process of change. Rest is never anything but apparent, or rather, relative. . . . *All reality is, therefore, tendency, if we agree to call tendency a nascent change of direction.*

Our mind, which seeks solid bases of operation, has as its principal function, in the ordinary course of life, to imagine *states* and *things*. Now and then it takes quasi-instantaneous views of the undivided mobility of the real. It thus obtains *sensations* and *ideas*. By that means it substitutes fixed points which mark a direction of change and tendency. This substitution is necessary to common sense, to language, to practical life, and even . . . to positive science. *Our intelligence, when it follows its natural inclination, proceeds by solid perceptions on the one hand, and by stable conceptions on the other.*[5]

We stabilize masses, particles large and small, out of vibrations, waves, intensities, so we can act upon and within them, rendering the mobile and the multiple provisionally unified and singular, framing the real through things as objects for us. We actively produce objects in the world, and in so doing, we make the world amenable to our actions but also render ourselves vulnerable to their reactions. This active making is part of our engagement in the world, the directive force of our perceptual and motor relations within the world. Our perception carves up the world and divides it into things. These things themselves are divisible, amenable to calculation and further subdivision; they are the result of a sort of subtraction: perception, intellect, cognition, and action reduce and refine the object, highlighting and isolating that which is of interest or potential relevance to our future action. To Bergson, the object is that cutting of the world that enables me to see how it meets my needs and interests: "The objects which surround my body reflect its possible action upon them."[6]

The separation between a thing and its environment cannot be absolutely definite and clear-cut; there is a passage by insensible gradations from the one to the other: the close solidarity which binds all the objects of the material universe, the perpetuality of their reciprocal actions and reactions, is sufficient to prove that they have not the precise limits which we attribute to them. Our perception outlines, so to speak, the form of their nucleus; it terminates them at the point where our possible action upon them ceases, where, consequently, they cease to interest our needs. Such is the primary and the most apparent operation of the perceiving mind: it marks out divisions in the continuity of the extended, simply following the suggestions of our requirements and the needs of practical life.[7]

This cutting of the world, this whittling down of the plethora of the world's interpenetrating qualities, those "pervading concrete extensity, *modifications, perturbations,* changes of *tension* or of *energy* and nothing else"[8] into objects amenable to our action is fundamentally a *constructive* process: we make the world of objects as an activity we undertake by living with and assimilating objects. We make objects in order to live in the world. Or, in another, Nietzschean sense, we must live in the world artistically, not as *homo sapiens* but as *homo faber:*

Let us start, then, from action, and lay down that the intellect aims, first of all, at constructing. This fabrication is exercised exclusively on inert matter, in this sense, that even if it makes use of organized material, it treats it as inert, without troubling about the life which animated it. And of inert matter itself, fabrication deals only with the solid; the rest escapes by its very fluidity. If, therefore, the tendency of the intellect is to fabricate, we may expect to find that whatever is fluid in the real will escape it in part, and whatever is life in the living will escape it altogether. *Our intelligence, as it leaves the hands of nature, has for its chief object the unorganized solid.*[9]

We cannot help but view the world in terms of solids, as things. But we leave behind something untapped of the fluidity of the world, the movements, vibrations, transformations that occur below the threshold of perception and calculation and outside the relevance of our practical concerns. Bergson suggests that we have other access to this rich profusion of vibrations that underlie the solidity of things.[10] Bergson describes these nonintellectual or extraintellectual impulses as instincts and intuitions, and while they are no more able to perceive the plethora of vibrations and processes that constitute the real, they are able to discern the interconnections, rather than the separations between things, to develop another perspective or interest in the division and production of the real. Intuition is our nonpragmatic, noneffective, nonexpedient relation to the world, the capacity we have to live in the world in excess of our needs, and in excess of the self-presentation or immanence of materiality, to collapse ourselves, as things, back into the world. Our "artisticness," as Nietzsche puts it, our creativity, in Bergsonian terms, consists in nothing else than the continuous experimentation with the world of things to produce new things from the fluidity or flux that eludes everyday need, or use value.

Technology and the Experimental
Technology, as human invention, is clearly one of the realms of "things" produced by and as the result of the

provocation of things-as-the-world. While things produce and are what is produced by the activities of life, things themselves are the object and project not only of the living but also of the technological. Technology is also a metaproduction: the production of things that produce things, a second-order production. Technology is in a sense the inevitable result of the encounter between life and matter, life and things, the consequence of the living's capacity to utilize the nonliving (and the living) *prosthetically*. Technology has existed as long as the human has; the primates' capacity for the use of found objects prefigures both the human and the technological. From the moment the human appears as such, it appears alongside of both artifacts and technologies, poesis and techne, which are the human's modes of evolutionary fitness, the compensations for its relative bodily vulnerability. According to Bergson, it is the propensity of instinct (in animals) and intelligence (in higher primates and man) to direct themselves to things, and thus to the making of things, and it is the status and nature of the instruments to which life is directed that distinguish the instincts from intelligence, yet connect them in a developmental continuum, with intelligence functioning as an elaboration of and deviation from instinct.[11]

Animals invent. They have instruments, which include their own body parts, as well as external objects. Humans produce technologies and especially, Bergson suggests, instruments that are detached and different from their own bodies, instruments that the body must learn to accommodate, instruments that transform both the thingness of things, and the body itself:

Invention becomes complete when it is materialized in a manufactured instrument. Towards that achievement the intelligence of animals tends as towards an ideal. . . . As regards human intel-

ligence, it has not been sufficiently noted that mechanical invention has been from the first its essential feature, that even to-day
our social life gravitates around the manufacture and use of artificial instruments, that the inventions which strew the road of
progress have also traced its direction. . . . In short, *intelligence,
considered in what seems to be its original feature, is the faculty of manufacturing artificial objects, especially tools to make tools, and of indefinitely varying the manufacture.*[12]

Technologies involve the invention of things that make
things, of second-order things. It is not that technologies
mediate between the human and the natural—for that is to
construe technology as somehow outside either the natural or the human (which today is precisely its misrepre-
sented place) instead of seeing it as the indefinite extension
of both the human and the natural and as their point of
overlap, the point of the conversion of the one into the
other, the tendency of nature to culture, and the cleaving
of culture to the stuff of nature. Rather, the technological
is the cultural construction of the thing that controls and
regulates other things: the correlate of the natural thing.
Pragmatism entails a recognition that the technological is
and always has been the condition of human action, as
necessary for us as things themselves, the cultural correlate of the thing, which is itself the human or living correlate of the world.

As Bergson acknowledges, while it is clumsy and
cumbersome relative to the instrumentality our bodies
provide us, technological invention does not succumb to a
preexistent function. Although technology is in a sense
made by us and for our purposes, it also performs a transformation on us: it increasingly facilitates not so much
better action but wider possibilities of acting, more action.
Technology is the great aid to action, for it facilitates, requires, and generates intelligence, which in turn radically

multiplies our possibilities of action, our instrumental and practical relation with the world: "The essential function of intelligence is . . . to see the way out of a difficulty in any circumstances whatever, to find what is most suitable, what answers best the question asked. Hence it bears essentially on the relations between a given situation and the means of utilizing it."[13] In an extraordinary passage, Bergson claims that the intellect transforms matter into things, which render them as prostheses, artificial organs, and, in a surprising reversal, simultaneously humanizes or *orders* nature, appends itself as a kind of prosthesis to inorganic matter itself, to function as its rational or conceptual supplement, its conscious rendering. Matter and life become reflections, through the ordering the intellect makes of the world. Things become the measure of life's action upon them, things become "standing reserve," life itself becomes extended through things:

All the elementary forces of the intellect tend to transform matter into an instrument of action, that is, in the etymological sense of the word, into an *organ*. Life, not content with producing organisms, would fain give them as an appendage inorganic matter itself, converted into an immense organ by the industry of the living being. Such is the initial task it assigns to intelligence. That is why the intellect always behaves as if it were fascinated by the contemplation of inert matter. It is life looking outward, adopting the ways of unorganized nature in principle, in order to direct them in fact.[14]

Inorganic matter, transformed into an immense organ, a prosthesis, is perhaps the primordial or elementary definition of architecture itself, which is, in a sense, the first prosthesis, the first instrumental use of intelligence to meld the world into things, through a certain primitive technicity, to fit the needs of the living. The inorganic becomes the mirror for the possible action of the living, the armature and architecture necessary for the survival and evolution of the living. Making, acting, functioning in the world, making oneself as one makes things—all these processes rely on and produce things as the correlate of the intellect, and leave behind the real out of which they were drawn and simplified.

Architecture and Making

What is left out in this process of making/reflecting is all that it is in matter, all that is outside the thing and outside technology: the flux of the real,[15] duration, vibration, contractions, and dilations, the multiplicity of the real, all that is not contained by the thing or by intellectual categories. The uncontained, the outside of matter, of things, of that which is not pragmatically available for use, is the object of different actions than that of intelligence and the technological. This outside, though, is not noumenal, outside all possible experience, but phenomenal, contained within it. It is simply that which is beyond the calculable, the framed or contained. It is the outside that architecture requires but cannot contain. Bergson understands this outside in a number of ways: as the real in its totality, as mobility, as movement, flux, duration, the virtual, the continuity which places the human within and as the material. What is now in question is the making of things, and that from which things are made, rather than the things made. This is what the rigorous process of intuition draws us toward, not things themselves so much as the teeming, suffuse network within which things are formed and outlined, the flux of the real.

This teeming flux of the real—"that continuity of becoming which is reality itself,"[16] the integration and unification of the most minute relations of matter so that they exist only by touching and interpenetrating, the flow and mutual investment of material relations into each other—must be symbolized, reduced to states, things, and numeration in order to facilitate practical action. This is not an error that we commit, a fault to be unlearned, but a condition of our continuing survival in the world. We could not function within this teeming multiplicity without some ability to skeletalize it, to diagram or simplify it. Yet this reduction and division occur only at a cost, which is the failure or inability of our scientific, representational, and linguistic systems to acknowledge the in-between of things, the plural interconnections that cannot be utilized or contained within and by things but that makes them possible. Things are solids, more and more minute in their constitution, as physics itself elaborates more and more minute fundamental particles:

Our intelligence is the prolongation of our senses. Before we speculate we must live, and life demands that we make use of matter, either with our organs, which are natural tools, or with tools, properly so-called, which are artificial organs. Long before there was a philosophy and a science, the role of intelligence was already that of manufacturing instruments and guiding the actions of our body on surrounding bodies. Science has pushed this labor of intelligence much further, but has not changed its direction. It aims above all at making us masters of matter.[17]

While the intellect masters that in the world which we need for our purposes, it is fundamentally incapable of understanding what in the world, in objects, and in us, is fluid, innumerable, outside calculation.[18] The limit of the intellect is the limit of the technical and the technological. The intellect functions to dissect, divide, atomize: contemporary binarization and digitalization are simply the current versions of this tendency to the clear-cut, the unambiguous, the oppositional or binary impulses of the intellect, which are bound by the impetus to (eventual or possible) actions. The technological, including and especially contemporary digital technologies, carries within it both the intellectual impulse to divide relations into solids and entities, objects or things, ones and zeros, and the living impulse to render the world practically amenable. Digitization translates, retranscribes, and circumscribes the fluidity and flux by decomposing the analog or the continuous—currents—into elements, packages, or units, represented by the binary code, and then recomposing them through addition: analysis then synthesis. But these processes of recomposition lose something in the process, although they reproduce themselves perfectly. The sweep and spontaneity of the curve, represented only through the aid of smaller and smaller grids, or the musical performance represented only through the discrete elements of the score, represent a diminution of the fullness of the real; the analog continuum is broken down and simplified in digitization.[19] What is lost in the process of digitization, in the scientific push to analysis or decomposition, is precisely the continuity, the force, that binds together the real as complexity and entwinement:

Suppose our eyes [were] made [so] that they cannot help seeing in the work of the master [painter] a mosaic effect. Or suppose our intellect [were] so made that it cannot explain the appearance of the figure on the canvas except as a work of mosaic. We should then be able to speak simply of a collection of little squares. . . . In neither case should we have got at the real process, for there are no squares brought together. It is the picture, i.e., the simple act, projected on the canvas, which, by the mere fact of entering our perception, is *de*composed before our eyes into thousands and thousands of little squares which present, as *re*composed, a wonderful arrangement.[20]

This is a prescient image of digitization: the recomposition of the whole through its decomposition into pixel-like units, the one serving as the representation of the other. The curve, the continuous stroke, the single movement of an arm, is certainly able to be decomposed into as many stops or breaks as one chooses: "A very small element of a curve is very near being a straight line. And the smaller it is, the nearer. In the limit, it may be termed a part of the curve or a part of the straight line, as you please, for in each of its points a curve coincides with its tangent."[21] But something of the curve or movement is lost when it is recomposed of its linear elements or grids, when the parts are added together—the simplicity and unity, the nondecomposable quality, disappears, to be replaced by immense complexity, that is, the duration of the movement disappears into its reconfiguration as measurable and reconfigurable space, object, or movement.

The thing and the body are correlates: both are artificial or conventional, pragmatic conceptions, cuttings, disconnections, that create a unity, continuity, and cohesion out of the plethora of interconnections that constitute the world. They mirror each other: the stability of one, the thing, is the guarantee of the stability and ongoing existence or viability of the other, the body. The thing is "made" for the body, made as manipulable for the body's needs. And the body is conceived on the model of the thing, equally knowable and manipulable by another body. This chain of connections is mutually confirming. The thing is the life of the body, and the body is that which unexpectedly occurs to things. Technology is that which ensures and continually refines the ongoing negotiations between bodies and things, the deepening investment of the one, the body, in the other, the thing.

Technology is not the supersession of the thing but its ever more entrenched functioning. The thing pervades technology, which is its extension, and also extends the human into the material. The task before us is not simply to make things or to resolve relations into things, more and more minutely framed and microscopically understood; rather, it may be to liberate matter from the constraint, the practicality, the utility of the thing, to orient technology not so much to knowing and mediating as to experience and the rich indeterminacy of duration. Instead of merely understanding the thing and the technologies it induces through intellect, perhaps we can also develop an acquaintance with things through intuition, that Bergsonian internal and intimate apprehension of the unique particularity of things, their constitutive interconnections, and the time within which things exist.[22]

The issue is not, of course, to abandon or even necessarily to criticize technologies, architecture, or the pragmatics of the thing, but rather, with Bergson, to understand both their limits and their residues. Perception, intellection, the thing, and the technologies they spawn proceed along the lines of practical action, and these require a certain primacy in day-to-day life. But they leave something out: the untapped, nonpractical, nonuseful, nonhuman, or extra-human continuity that is the object of intuition, of empirical attunement without means or ends.

One of the questions ahead of us now is this: What are the conditions of digitization and binarization? Can we produce technologies of other kinds? Is technology inherently simplification and reduction of the real? What in us is being extended and prosthetically rendered in technological development? Can other vectors be extended instead? What might a technology of processes, of intuition rather than things and practice, look like?

One **Embodying Space: An Interview**

This interview was conducted by Kim Armitage and Paul Dash on Wednesday, September 18, 1996, and was first published in *Aedon* 4, no. 1 (1996), 47–64.

1. See, in this volume, "Lived Spatiality."

2. See "Women, Chora, Dwelling," *ANY*, no. 4 (January-February 1994), 22–27.

Two **Lived Spatiality (The Spaces of Corporeal Desire)**

This essay was first published in Brian Boigon, ed., *Culture Lab* (New York: Princeton Architectural Press, 1993).

1. Sigmund Freud, "The Ego and the Id," in *The Standard Edition of the Complete Psychological Works of Sigmund Freud*, ed. James Strachey, vol. 19 (Oxford: Hogarth Press, 1953), 26.

2. Jacques Lacan, "Some Reflections on the Ego," *International Journal of Psychoanalysis*, no. 34 (1953), 13.

3. Roger Caillois, "Mimicry and Legendary Psychasthenia," *October*, no. 31 (1984), 25.

4. Ibid., 28.

5. Ibid., 30.

6. Ibid.

7. Michael Heim, "Re Metaphysics of Virtual Reality," in Sandra K. Helsel and Judith P. Roth, eds., *Virtual Reality: Theory, Practice and Promise* (London: Meckler, 1991), 3.

8. Howard Rheingold, *Virtual Reality* (New York: Summit Books, 1991), 191; emphasis added.

9. Ibid., 346.

Three **Futures, Cities, Architecture**

This essay was presented as a paper at the conference "Invisible Cities: From the Postmodern Metropolis to the Cities of the Future," New York City, October 1996.

Four **Architecture from the Outside**

This essay first appeared in Cynthia C. Davidson, ed., *Anyplace* (Cambridge: MIT Press, 1995), and was reprinted in my book *Space, Time and Perversion: Essays on the Politics of Bodies* (New York: Routledge, 1995).

1. Brian Massumi, in his rewarding *A User's Guide to Capitalism and Schizophrenia: Deviations from Deleuze and Guattari* (Cambridge: MIT Press, 1992), characterizes nomad thought in the following terms: "'Nomad thought' does not lodge itself in the edifice of an ordered interiority; it moves freely in an element of exteriority. It does not repose on identity; it rides difference. It does not respect the artificial division between the three domains of representation, subject, concept and being; it replaces restrictive analogy with a conductivity that knows no bounds. . . . Rather than reflecting the world [the concepts it creates] are immersed in a changing state of things. A concept is a brick. It can be used to build the courthouse of reason. Or it can be thrown through the window" (5).

2. The bizarre reading is based on the use and inherent ambiguity of the building metaphor in the philosophical tradition. De-*construction* and post*structuralism* lend themselves to an architectural appropriation insofar as they are already appropriated from architecture. The architectonic remains a guiding philosophical ideal.

3. Deleuze frequently compares geography to history, and privileges the former for its amenability to concepts of movement, direction, and change: "We think too much in terms of history, whether personal or universal. Becomings belong to geography, they are orientations, directions, entries and exits." (Gilles Deleuze and Claire Parnet, *Dialogues*, trans. Hugh Tomlinson and Barbara Habberjam [New York: Columbia University Press,

1987], 3.) He links history to the sedentary and the functioning of the State, while geography is nomadic: "History is always written from the sedentary point of view and in the name of a unitary State apparatus, at least a possible one, even when the topic is nomads. What is lacking is a Nomadology, the opposite of a history." (Gilles Deleuze and Félix Guattari, *A Thousand Plateaus: Capitalism and Schizophrenia*, trans. Brian Massumi [Minneapolis: University of Minnesota Press, 1983], 23.)

4. As developed in Gilles Deleuze, *The Fold: Leibniz and the Baroque*, trans. Tom Conley (Minneapolis: University of Minnesota Press, 1993).

5. This is one of many notions Deleuze uses as a scattergun in rethinking transgression: not how to stutter in language, but how to make language itself stutter: "It is when the language system overstrains itself that it begins to stutter, to murmur, or to mumble, then the entire language reaches the limit that sketches the outside and confronts silence. When the language system is so much strained, language suffers a pressure that delivers it to silence." Gilles Deleuze, *Difference and Repetition*, trans. Paul Patton (New York: Columbia University Press, 1994), 28.

6. For two non-jargon-filled architecturally oriented projects that utilize Deleuze's work without applying it, see Meaghan Morris, "Great Moments in Social Climbing: King Kong and the Human Fly," in Beatriz Colomina, ed., *Sexuality and Space* (New York: Princeton Architectural Press, 1992), 1–51; and John Rajchman, "Lightness: A Concept in Architecture" and "The Earth Is Called Light," both in *ANY* 5 (1994).

7. See, for example, Rex Butler and Paul Patton, "Dossier on Gilles Deleuze," *Agenda: Contemporary Art Magazine* 33 (September 1993), 16–36.

8. This process is already under way with talk now of the building as envelope—a metaphor that in fact should acknowledge a debt to Irigaray even more than to Deleuze, whose project is only peripherally related to enveloping and envelopment. See Peter Eisenman, "Folding in Time: The Singularity of Rebstock," *Columbia Documents of Architecture and Theory: D* 2 (1993), 99–112.

9. Deleuze, *Difference and Repetition*, 139.

10. Deleuze distinguishes the problem from the theorem insofar as the latter contains within itself its own consequences while the problem is inherently open: "The problematic is distinguished from the theorematic (or constructivism from the axiomatic) in that the theorem develops internal relationships from principle to consequences, while the problem introduces an event from the outside—the removal, addition, cutting—which constitutes its own conditions and determines the 'case' or cases. . . . This outside of the problem is not reducible to the exteriority of the physical world any more than to the psychological interiority of a thinking ego." Gilles Deleuze, *Cinema 2: The Time-Image*, trans. Hugh Tomlinson and Robert Galeta (Minneapolis: University of Minnesota Press, 1993), 174–175.

11. "Artaud says that the problem (for him) was not to orientate his thought, or to perfect the expression of what he thought, or to acquire application and method or to perfect his poems, but simply to manage to think something. For him, this is the only conceivable 'work': it presupposes an impulse, a compulsion to think which passes though all sorts of bifurcations, spreading from the nerves and being communicated to the soul in order to arrive at thought. Henceforth, thought is also forced to think its central collapse, its fracture, its own natural 'powerlessness' which is indistinguishable from the greatest power—in other words, from those unformulated forces, the cogitanda, as though from so many thefts or trespasses in thought." Deleuze, *Difference and Repetition*, 147.

12. As Rajchman puts it, in a related point raised in a different context: "A concept . . . has an open-ended relation to design. It tries to free a new complex, which serves, as it were, as a 'strange attractor' to certain features or strategies, assembling them in new ways. To do this, it must itself become complex, inventing a space of free connection to other concepts. 'A concept is never simple,' Jean Nouvel says, taking up in architecture a phrase from Gilles Deleuze. It is connected to others in a kind of force field that serves to displace the current doxa, stimulating thinking to go off

in other directions, or inviting one to think in other ways." Rajch-man, "Lightness," 5.

13. Deleuze, *Difference and Repetition*, 139.

14. The first illusion consists in thinking difference in terms of the identity of the concept or the subject, the illusion of identity; the second illusion is the subordination of difference to resemblance (which is linked by Deleuze to various strategies of equalization and assimilation); the third is the strategy of tying difference to negation (which has the effect of reducing difference to disparateness); and fourth, the subordination of difference to the analogy of judgment (which disseminates difference according to rules of distribution). See Deleuze, *Difference and Repetition*, 265–270.

15. "The virtual is the *unsaid* of the statement, the unthought of thought. It is real and subsists in them, but must be forgotten at least momentarily for a clear statement to be produced as evaporative surface effect. . . . The task of philosophy is to explore that inevitable forgetting, to reattach statements to their conditions of emergence." Massumi, *A User's Guide*, 46.

16. "Between Heidegger and Artaud, Maurice Blanchot was able to give the fundamental question of what makes us think, what forces us to think, back to Artaud; what forces us to think is 'the inpower [*impouvoir*] of thought,' the figure of nothingness, the inexistence of the whole which could be thought. What Blanchot diagnoses everywhere in literature is particularly clear in cinema: on the one hand the presence of an unthinkable in thought, which would be both its source and barrier; on the other hand the presence to infinity of another thinker, who shatters every monologue of a thinking self." Deleuze, *Cinema 2*, 167–168.

17. Gilles Deleuze, *Foucault*, trans. Seán Hand (Minneapolis: University of Minnesota Press, 1988), 326.

18. Ibid., 97.

19. Ibid., 98.

20. Deleuze, *Cinema 2*, 175.

21. Significantly, elsewhere in the same text, Deleuze instead wants to equate the outside with force: "Forces always come from the outside, from an outside that is farther away than any form of exteriority" (*Cinema 2*, 122). Does this mean that thought and force can be equated? There is some plausibility to this claim, given Deleuze's "activist" understanding of thought; moreover, such a reading would enable the Nietzschean distinction between the forces of action and reaction that Deleuze develops in *Nietzsche and Philosophy* (trans. Hugh Tomlinson; New York: Columbia University Press, 1983) to apply directly to thought itself. It is clear that Deleuze is advocating an active thought, thinking that is productive and self-expanding.

22. Deleuze posits the outside of thought as life itself, as the impetus and resistance of life to categories, and its push beyond them. In *Cinema 2* he wants to link the unthought to the body itself, which can no longer be conceived as a medium of thought or a blockage to it (as in the Platonic and Cartesian traditions): rather, the body is the *motive* of thought, its source or well: "The body is no longer the obstacle that separates thought from itself, that which it has to overcome to reach thinking. It is on the contrary that which it plunges into or must plunge into, in order to reach the unthought, that is life. Not that the body thinks, but, obstinate and stubborn, it forces us to think, and forces us to think what is concealed from thought, life. Life will no longer be made to appear before the categories of thought; thought will be thrown into the categories of life. The categories of life are precisely the attitudes of the body, its postures. 'We do not even know what a body can do': in its sleep, in its drunkenness, in its efforts and resistances. To think is to learn what a non-thinking body is capable of, its capacity, its postures" (189).

23. Deleuze, *Cinema 2*, 116.

24. Massumi, *A User's Guide*, 99.

25. "What counts is . . . the interstices between images [in cinema], between two images: a spacing which means that each image is plucked from the void and falls back into it." Deleuze, *Cinema 2*, 179.

26. Deleuze's own explanation of the movements and speeds of becoming continually emphasizes the ways becoming-other refuses imitation or analogy, refuses to represent itself as like something else: rather, becoming is the activation or freeing of lines, forces, and intensities from the boundaries and constraints of an identity or fixed purpose to the transformation and problematization of identity: "An Eskimo-becoming . . . does not consist in playing the Eskimo, in imitating or identifying yourself with him [sic] or taking the Eskimo upon yourself, but in assembling something between you and him, for you can only become Eskimo if the Eskimo himself becomes something else. The same goes for lunatics, drug addicts, alcoholics. . . . We are trying to extract from madness the life which it contains, while hating the lunatics who constantly kill life, turn it against itself. We are trying to extract from alcohol the life which it contains, without drinking." Deleuze and Parnet, *Dialogues*, 53.

27. Massumi says it much better than I am able to: "A crack has opened in habit, a 'zone of indeterminacy' is glimpsed in the hyphen between the stimulus and the response. Thought consists in widening that gap, filling it fuller and fuller with potential responses, to the point that, confronted with a particular stimulus, the body's reaction cannot be predicted. Thought-in-becoming is less a willful act than an undoing: the nonaction of suspending established stimulus-response circuits to create a zone where chance and change may intervene." Massumi, *A User's Guide*, 99.

28. Constantin Boundas, in his introduction to *The Deleuze Reader* (New York: Columbia University Press, 1993), suggests a close convergence between Derrida's notion of supplementarity and Deleuze's understanding of the outside, which seems to capture the spirit in which there may be a political allegiance between them, in spite of the question of the (possible) incommensurability of their theoretical concerns: "The outside is not another site, but rather an out-of-site that erodes and dissolves all the other sites. Its logic, therefore, is like the logic of difference, provided that the latter is understood in its transcendental and not in its empirical dimension; instead of difference between x and y, we must now conceive the difference of x from itself. Like the

structure of supplementarity whose logic it follows, the outside is never exhausted; every attempt to capture it generates an excess or supplement that in turn feeds anew the flows of deterritorialization, and releases new lines of flight. . . . The outside is Deleuze-Leibniz's virtual that is always more than the actual; it is the virtual that haunts the actual and, as it haunts it, makes it flow and change" (15).

Five Cyberspace, Virtuality, and the Real: Some Architectural Reflections

This essay was published in Cynthia C. Davidson, ed., *Anybody* (Cambridge: MIT Press, 1997).

1. For a series of detailed and influential definitions/explanations of the concept of cyberspace, see Michael Benedikt, *Cyberspace: First Steps* (Cambridge: MIT Press, 1991), 2.

2. Randall Walser, quoted in Howard Rheingold, *Virtual Reality* (New York: Summit Books, 1991), 191.

3. In his *City of Bits: Space, Place, and the Infobahn* (Cambridge: MIT Press, 1995), 44, William J. Mitchell seems to confuse the status of virtual sound in his characterization of the Walkman as an instrument of virtuality. There is nothing virtual about the Walkman, at least not compared to the reality of the CD or the cassette, the radio or the telephone. The more relevant distinction here is between the public and private order of sound: the telephone and Walkman privatize what would have been inherently public sounds; they do not veil over, displace, or remove real sound: "When you wear your Walkman on the bus, your feet are on the floor and your eyes see the physical enclosure, but an electronic audio environment masks the immediately surrounding one and your eyes are in another place. . . . When you don a head-mounted stereo display to play *Dactyl Nightmare* in a virtual reality arcade, the immediate visual environment is supplanted by virtual space, but your sense of touch reminds you that you still remain surrounded by now-invisible-solid objects."

Mitchell ascribes to the virtual visual environment a capacity to supplant the visuality of the real that he cannot attribute to electronically generated sound. Electronic sound, even prosthetically implanted in the organic body (hearing aids long predate the Walkman, which itself is clearly a transitional stage in the increasing miniaturization of aural prostheses), even simulated or synthesized sound, has no dimension of displacement, illusion, masking. It is sound qua indefinitely reproducible; it may be the reproduction of sound originally made elsewhere or with no natural origin, but it lacks the phantasmatic dimensions of a virtual visuality, even the phantasmatic aspirations of virtual touch.

4. I am indebted to Geoffrey Batchen for this point: "According to Lacan's description of the mirror stage, our unconscious efforts to incorporate a perceived difference between real and virtual results in our becoming an irretrievable split being, a creature always divided from itself." Batchen, "Spectres of Cyberspace," *Afterimage* 23, no. 3 (November-December 1995), 7.

5. See Gilles Deleuze, *Bergsonism*, trans. Hugh Tomlinson and Barbara Habberjam (New York: Zone, 1988); and Deleuze, *Cinema 2: The Time-Image*, trans. Hugh Tomlinson and Robert Galeta (Minneapolis: University of Minnesota Press, 1989).

6. The technological form of VR is still uncertain. There seem to be two approaches: X-ray spectacles or *Star Trek*'s Holodeck, basically clothes or architecture. See Stephen Bingham, interview by Brian Boigon and David Clarkson, "The Key to Cybercity: Stephen Bingham," *M5V* 2 (Winter 1991–1992), 27.

7. Benedikt, introduction to *Cyberspace: First Steps*, 4 (my emphasis).

8. Marcos Novak, "Liquid Architecture in Cyberspace," in Benedikt, *Cyberspace: First Steps*, 228.

9. Allucquère Roseanne Stone, "Virtual Systems," in Jonathan Crary and Sanford Kwinter, eds., *Incorporations* (New York: Zone, 1992), 610.

10. Novak, "Liquid Architecture in Cyberspace," 241.

11. Elizabeth Grosz, *Volatile Bodies: Toward a Corporeal Feminism* (Bloomington: Indiana University Press, 1994).

Six **In-Between: The Natural in Architecture and Culture**

This essay was presented as a paper at the conference "Constructing Identity: Between Architecture and Culture," Cornell University, October 1997.

1. Gilbert Simondon, "The Genesis of the Individual," trans. Mark Cohen and Sanford Kwinter, in Jonathan Crary and Sanford Kwinter, eds., *Incorporations* (New York: Zone Books, 1992), 311–312.

2. Elizabeth Grosz, "Bodies/Cities," in *Space, Time and Perversion: Essays on the Politics of Bodies* (New York: Routledge, 1995).

3. For a current overview of the role of computer simulation and what has been called "artificial societies," see Nigel Gilbert and Rosaria Conte, eds., *Artificial Societies: The Computer Simulation of Social Life* (London: University College London Press, 1995).

4. Gilles Deleuze and Félix Guattari, *A Thousand Plateaus: Capitalism and Schizophrenia*, trans. Brian Massumi (Minneapolis: University of Minnesota Press, 1987), 3.

Seven **The Future of Space: Toward an Architecture of Invention**

This essay was first published in Cynthia C. Davidson, ed., *Anyhow* (Cambridge: MIT Press, 1998).

1. Such a continuum—the space-time of contemporary science—always derives from a more primordial understanding of time and space: this was Henri Bergson's critique of Albert Einstein in *Duration and Simultaneity* (trans. Leon Jacobson; Manchester: Clinamen Books, 1999). It is not clear to me, however, that access to this more primordial space and time is provided, as Bergson suggested, by experience.

2. Jacques Derrida, "Différance," in *Margins of Philosophy*, trans. Alan Bass (Chicago: University of Chicago Press, 1982), 13.

3. Henri Bergson, *Matter and Memory*, trans. N. M. Paul and W. S. Palmer (New York: Zone Books, 1988), 206.

4. Ibid., 217.

5. Gilles Deleuze, *Bergsonism*, trans. Hugh Tomlinson and Barbara Habberjam (New York: Zone Books, 1988), 87.

6. Bergson, *Matter and Memory*, 187.

7. Ibid., 231.

8. Ibid., 68.

9. Ibid.

10. See figure 5, Bergson, *Matter and Memory*, 162:

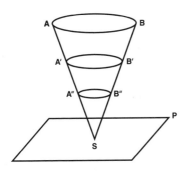

The cone SAB represents the totality of memory, in its different degrees of contraction. The base AB is situated in the past and is unable to link with the present, while the point S indicates my continuing present. The plane P is my actual present representation of the universe. S is the locus of the sensorimotor functions. The segments AB, A'B', and A''B'' are repetitions of memory more or less compressed. The more expansive and detailed, the less accessible is memory to present action.

11. Bergson, *Matter and Memory*, 57.

12. This example is already an indication of the strangely postmodernist, indeed surprisingly posthuman character of Bergson's writings, even those characterized as the most committed to humanism. Indeed, Bergson's own wayward, quiet peculiarity and complexity compared to the simplified characterizations generally used now to discount his work seem to attract Deleuze's

bastardized, anal reading: "Bergson is not one of those philosophers who ascribes a properly human wisdom and equilibrium to philosophy. To open us up to the inhuman and the superhuman (*durations* which are inferior or superior to our own), to go beyond the human condition: This is the meaning of philosophy, in so far as our condition condemns us to live among badly analyzed composites, and to be badly analyzed composites ourselves." Deleuze, *Bergsonism*, 28.

13. Deleuze, *Bergsonism*, 59.

14. Bergson, *Matter and Memory*, 171.

15. Deleuze, *Bergsonism*, 99.

16. "This time-image extends naturally into a language-image, and a thought-image. What the past is to time, sense is to language and idea to thought. Sense as past of language is the form of its pre-existence, that which we place ourselves in at once in order to understand images of sentences, to distinguish the images of words and even phonemes that we hear. It is therefore organized in coexisting circles, sheets or regions, between which we choose according to actual auditory signs which are grasped in a confused way. Similarly, we place ourselves initially in the idea; we jump into one of its circles in order to form images which correspond to the actual quest." Deleuze, *Bergsonism*, 99–100.

17. Ibid., 61–62.

18. Ibid., 97.

19. Constantin Boundas states this well: "Virtualities generate disjunctions as they begin to actualize the tendencies which were contained in the original unity and compossibility. Differenciation does not happen between one actual term and another actual term in a homogeneously unilinear series, but rather between a virtual term and the heterogeneous terms which actualize it along the lines of flight of several ramified series." Constantin V. Boundas, "Bergson-Deleuze: An Ontology of the Virtual," in Paul Patton, ed., *Deleuze: A Critical Reader* (Oxford: Blackwell Books, 1996), 81–106.

Eight **Embodied Utopias: The Time of Architecture**

An earlier version of this essay was presented at the conference "Embodied Utopias," University of Chicago, 1997.

1. Plato, *The Republic*, trans. G. M. Gude (Indianapolis: Hackett Publishing, 1974), 499b, p. 155.

2. Thomas More, *Utopia* (Cambridge: Cambridge University Press, 1975), Book 1, 16.

3. While More insists on the equality of all, the equal access of all to material goods, and the refusal of private property, he also refers to slaves and bondsmen, to those chained or not citizens. Like that of all liberal and egalitarian theorists, More's equality is made possible only because of the unacknowledged and unpaid labor of the noncitizen, the socially excluded and unequal: "Bondsmen do the slaughtering and cleaning in these places [outside the city limits]: citizens are not allowed to do such work" (*Utopia*, Book 2, 57).

4. "Utopia is the space where the contradictory inheritance of the Enlightenment appears in one of its clearest terms. Utopias, while not invented in the Enlightenment, certainly flourished in the eighteenth century and persisted into the nineteenth century, when a number of socialist and socialist-feminist utopias proliferated. . . . But by the twentieth century, the problems of implementing the ideal state or community have become so obvious that the more characteristic and certainly the best-known form of the genre would seem to be dystopic: Zamyatin's *We*, Aldous Huxley's *Brave New World*, George Orwell's *1984*." Margaret Whitford, *Luce Irigaray: Philosophy in the Feminine* (London: Routledge, 1991), 18.

5. Michèle Le Doeuff presents a slightly different understanding of the atopic; while she concurs with the indeterminacy and ambiguity of the term, she wants to link it to an as yet uninformed audience: what distinguishes a utopic from an atopic discourse is the ambiguity of its mode of address:

> *Atopos* means that which has no place, but also that which is bizarre, extravagant or strange. An atopia is a text which cannot immediately be given one single correct meaning by

its reader. . . . A work is atopian if it finds no circle of witnesses or readers already able to receive it. That is to say, also, that it manifests its author's singularity. The text is his own (and he further asserts his mastery of the work by retrieving it into univocity, by operating a reprise of his text) and is shareable only at the cost of a series of mediations.

Le Doeuff, "The Polysemy of Atopian Discourse," in *The Philosophical Imaginary*, trans. Colin Gordon (Stanford: Stanford University Press, 1989), 54–55.

For Le Doeuff, though her point is not merely semantic or classificatory, this means that Plato, More, Bacon, Rousseau, and others, must be considered more atopic than utopic. As an example of utopic thinking, she cites Marx and Engels, for whom the structure of self-justificatory writing seems irrelevant: "Marx and Engels do not have to provide instructions for the use of the *Communist Manifesto*. Its political meaning is clear: that is to say, already shared by the group it addresses, the activists of the Communist League. Moreover Marx and Engels do not present themselves as its authors, but as spokesmen. All these factors go together" (ibid., 55).

While I would agree with Le Doeuff's distinction between texts that attempt to contain their own polysemy and those which do not, nonetheless, a different distinction needs to be drawn for my purposes here: there is a significant difference between those discourses that provide concrete images of an ideal future (from Plato to Marx and contemporary feminism), and those discourses that, while directed to a future preferable to our present, refuse to characterize or represent its concrete features (Nietzsche, Deleuze, Irigaray), and can only specify elements it would *not* contain.

6. See Michel Foucault, "The Discourse on Language," in *The Archaeology of Knowledge* (New York: Harper Colophon, 1972).

7. Le Doeuff, "The Polysemy of Atopian Discourse," 48–49.

8. See Elizabeth Grosz, "The Future of Space," in this volume.

9. See my discussion in "The Future of Space" of Bergson's concept of the past. As Deleuze suggests: "The past and the present

do not denote two successive moments, but two elements which coexist: One is the present, which does not cease to pass, and the other is the past, which does not cease to be but through which all presents pass. . . . The past does not follow the present, but on the contrary, is presupposed by it as the pure condition without which it would not pass. In other words, each present goes back to itself as past." Gilles Deleuze, *Bergsonism*, trans. Hugh Tomlinson and Barbara Habberjam (New York: Zone Books, 1988), 59.

10. This timelessness is what More shares with Plato: "So I reflect on the wonderfully wise and sacred institutions of the Utopians, who are so well governed by so few laws. Among them virtue has its rewards, yet everything is shared equally, and all men live in plenty. I contrast them with the many other nations, none of which, though all are constantly passing new ordinances, can ever order its affairs satisfactorily." More, *Utopia*, Book 1, 38.

11. Plato, *Republic*, 456e.

12. Ibid., 456d.

13. More, *Utopia*, Book 2, 82–83.

14. Cf. More's description of cooking and eating arrangements: "Planning the meal, as well as preparing and cooking food, is carried out by the women alone, with each family taking its turn. . . . The men sit with their backs to the wall, the women on the outside, so that if a woman has a sudden qualm or pain, such as occasionally happens during pregnancy, she may get up without disturbing the others, and go off to the nurses." More, *Utopia*, Book 2, 58.

15. See here Irigaray's *Speculum of the Other Woman*, trans. Gillian C. Gill (Ithaca: Cornell University Press, 1985), and *This Sex Which Is Not One*, trans. Catherine Porter with Carolyn Burke (Ithaca: Cornell University Press, 1985).

16. This is Margaret Whitford's claim in her reading of Irigaray. See Whitford, *Luce Irigaray*, especially 18–20.

17. Irigaray, quoted in ibid., 14.

This essay was first published in Cynthia C. Davidson, ed., *Anymore* (Cambridge: MIT Press, 2000).

1. Alphonso Lingis, *The Community of Those Who Have Nothing in Common* (Bloomington: Indiana University Press, 1994), 12.

2. René Girard has presented highly persuasive arguments to suggest that the structure of the scapegoat provides a means by which social collectives retain their cohesion during times of crisis. The scapegoat is the one, marked by some difference, onto whom the violence of the group is enacted and through whose sacrifice the group resolves its own internal differences and impulses to violence:

> The signs that indicate a victim's selection result not from the difference within the system but from the differences outside the system, the potential for the system to differ from its own difference, in other words, not to be different at all, to cease to exist as a system. This is easily seen in the case of physical disabilities. The human body is a system of anatomic differences. If a disability, even as the result of an accident, is disturbing, it is because it gives the impression of a disturbing dynamism. It seems to threaten the very system. Efforts to limit it are unsuccessful; it disturbs the differences that surround it. These in turn become *monstrous*, rush together, are compressed and blended together to the point of destruction. Difference that exists outside the system is terrifying because it reveals the truth of the system, its relativity, its fragility, and its mortality.

René Girard, *The Scapegoat* (Baltimore: Johns Hopkins University Press, 1986), 21.

3. Georges Bataille, "The Notion of Expenditure," in *Visions of Excess: Selected Writings 1927–1939*, ed. and trans. Allan Stoekl (Manchester: University of Manchester Press, 1985), 118.

4. Bataille links the tall exotic skyscraper with the Tower of Babel, and with the oedipal struggle between father and son:

We find here an attempt to climb to the sky—that is to say, to dethrone the father, to possess oneself of his virility—followed by the destruction of the rebels: castration of the son by his father, whose rival he is. Furthermore, the coupling, rash though it may be, of these two words, the verb "scrape" on the one hand, and, on the other, the substantive "sky," immediately evokes an erotic image in which the building, which scrapes, is a phallus even more explicit than the Tower of Babel, and the sky is scraped—the object of desire of the said phallus—is the incestuously desired mother, as she is in all attempts at the spoliation of the paternal virility.

Georges Bataille, "Skyscraper," in *Encyclopædia Acephalica: Comprising the Critical Dictionary and Related Texts edited by Georges Bataille and the Encyclopædia Da Costa*, ed. Robert Lebel and Isabelle Waldberg (London: Atlas Press, 1995), 69–72.

5. Georges Bataille, "Architecture," in *Encyclopædia Acephalica*, 35–36.

6. Ibid., 35.

7. Ibid., 36.

8. "When in a dream a diamond signifies excrement, it is not only a question of association by contrast; in the unconscious, jewels, like excrement, are cursed matter that flows from a wound: they are a part of oneself destined for open sacrifice (they serve, in fact, as sumptuous gifts charged with sexual love)." Bataille, "The Notion of Expenditure," 119.

9. Luce Irigaray, *An Ethics of Sexual Difference*, trans. Carolyn Burke and Gillian C. Gill (Ithaca: Cornell University Press, 1993), 7.

10. As Luce Irigaray claims:

In the beginning there was space and the creation of space, as is said in all theogonies. The gods, God, first create *space*. And time is there, more or less in the service of space. On the first day, the first days, the gods, God, make a world by separating the elements. This world is then peopled, and a rhythm is established among its inhabitants. God would be time itself, lavishing or exteriorizing itself in its actions in space, in places.

Philosophy then confirms the genealogy of the task of the gods of God. Time becomes the *interiority* of the subject itself, and space, its *exteriority* (this problematic is developed by Kant in the *Critique of Pure Reason*). The subject, the master of time, becomes the axis of the world's ordering, with its something beyond the moment and eternity: God. He effects the passage between time and space.

Irigaray, *An Ethics of Sexual Difference*, 7.

11. "If traditionally, and as a mother, woman represents *place* for man, such a limit means that she becomes a *thing*, with some possibility of change from one historical period to another. She finds herself delineated as a thing. Moreover, the maternal-feminine also serves as an *envelope*, a *container*, the starting point from which man limits his things. The *relationship between envelope and things* constitutes one of the aporias, or the aporia, of Aristotelianism and of the philosophical systems derived from it." Irigaray, *An Ethics of Sexual Difference*, 10.

12. Ibid., 11.

13. Ibid.

14. Luce Irigaray, "Où et comment habiter?" *Les Cahiers du Grif* 26 (March 1983), 23. Issue on *Jouir*.

15. Ibid., 27.

16. In her commentary on Aristotle's *Physics*, Book IV, Irigaray argues that place is a maternal containment for the object that it houses: "It seems that a fetus would be in a place. And man's penis for as long as it is inside the woman. Woman is in the house, but this is not the same type of place as a living bodily site. On the other hand, place, in her, is in place, not only as organs but as vessel or receptacle. It is place twice over: as mother and as woman." Irigaray, *An Ethics of Sexual Difference*, 52.

17. Ibid.

Ten **The Thing**

This essay will appear in Cynthia C. Davidson, ed., *Anything* (Cambridge: MIT Press, forthcoming).

1. See, for example, Hanna Fenichel Pitkin's curiously titled *The Attack of the Blob: Hannah Arendt's Concept of the Social* (Chicago: University of Chicago Press, 1998).

2. As William James implies in his discussion of the thing, or object, the object is that which has effects, directly or indirectly, on our perceptual responses and motor behavior. The object is the ongoing possibility of perception and action, the virtual trigger for responsiveness: "To attain perfect clearness in our thoughts of an object, then, we need only consider what conceivable effects of a practical kind the object may involve—what sensations we are to expect from it, and what reactions we must prepare. Our conception of these effects, whether immediate or remote, is then for us the whole of our conception of the object, so far as that conception has positive significance at all." William James, "What Pragmatism Means," in *Pragmatism and Four Essays from The Meaning of Truth* (Cleveland: Meridian Books, 1970), 43.

3. William James, "Pragmatism and Humanism," in ibid., 165.

4. William James, "Pragmatism and Common Sense," in ibid., 118–119.

5. Henri Bergson, *The Creative Mind: An Introduction to Metaphysics*, trans. Mabell L. Andison (New York: Citadel Press, 1992), 223.

6. Henri Bergson, *Matter and Memory*, trans. N. M. Paul and W. S. Palmer (New York: Zone Books, 1988), 21.

7. Ibid., 209–210.

8. Ibid., 201.

9. Henri Bergson, *Creative Evolution*, trans. Arthur Mitchell (New York: Random House, 1944), 153.

10. Indeed, Bergson's discussion of William James's pragmatism in *The Creative Mind* (see "On the Pragmatism of William James")

indicates that James's notion of truth is itself an acknowledgment of the limit of knowledge rather than its pervasiveness:

> The definition that James gives to truth, therefore, is an integral part of his conception of reality. If reality is not that economic and systematic universe our logic likes to imagine, if it is not sustained by a framework of intellectuality, intellectual truth is a human invention whose effect is to utilize reality rather than to enable us to penetrate it. And if reality does not form a single whole, if it is multiple and mobile, made up of cross-currents, truth which arises from contact with one of these currents,—truth felt before being conceived,—is more capable of seizing and storing up reality than truth merely thought. (259)

11. Bergson suggests that instinct finds a kind of technology ready at hand in the body and its organs, in found objects whose use is instinctively dictated, and in the differential dispersal of instinctual capacities in social animals that are highly stratified, as many insects are. Intelligence, on the other hand, invents and makes technology, but it also diverts natural objects into technological products through their unexpected and innovative use:

> Instinct perfected is a faculty of using and even of constructing organizing instruments; intelligence perfected is the faculty of making and using unorganized instruments.
>
> The advantages and drawbacks of these two modes of activity are obvious. Instinct finds the appropriate instrument at hand: this instrument, which makes and repairs itself, which presents, like all the works of nature, an infinite complexity of detail combined with a marvelous simplicity of function, does at once, when required, what it is called upon to do, without difficulty and with a perfection that is often wonderful. In return, it retains an almost invariable structure, since a modification of it involves a modification of the species. . . . The instrument constructed intelligently, on the contrary, is an imperfect instrument. It costs an effort. It is generally troublesome to handle. But, as it is made of unorganized matter, it can take any form whatsoever, serve any purpose, free the living being from every new difficulty that

arises and bestow on it an unlimited number of powers. Whilst it is inferior to the natural instrument for the satisfaction of immediate wants, its advantage over it is greater, the less urgent the need. Above all, it reacts on the nature of the being that constructs it; for in calling on him to exercise a new function, it confers on him, so to speak, a richer organization, being an artificial organ by which the natural organism is extended. For every need that it satisfies, it creates a new need; and so, instead of closing, like instinct, the round of action within which the animal tends to move automatically, it lays open to activity an unlimited field into which it is driven further and further, and made more and more free.

Bergson, *Creative Evolution*, 140–141.

12. Ibid., 138–139 (emphasis in original).

13. Ibid., 150–151.

14. Ibid., 161.

15. Ibid., 250.

16. Bergson, *Matter and Memory*, 139.

17. Bergson, *The Creative Mind*, 43.

18. Bergson writes:

We shall never explain by means of particles, whatever these may be, the simple properties of matter. . . . This is precisely the object of chemistry. It studies *bodies* rather than *matter*; and so we understand why it stops at the atom, which is still endowed with the general properties of matter. But the materiality of the atom dissolves more and more under the eyes of the physicist. We have no reason, for instance, for representing the atom to ourselves as a solid, rather than as a liquid or gaseous, nor for picturing the reciprocal action of atoms as shocks rather than in any other way. Why do we think of a solid atom, and why do we think of shocks? Because solids, being the bodies on which we clearly have the most hold, are those which interest us most in our relations with the external world, and because contact is the only means which appears to be at our disposal in order to make our body act upon other bodies. But very simple experiments show that there is never true contact between two neighboring bodies, and besides, solidity is far from being an absolutely defined state of matter. Solidity and shock borrow, then, their apparent clearness from the habits and necessities of practical life.

Bergson, *Matter and Memory*, 199.

19. On the distinction between the analog and the digital, see an early piece by Anthony Wilden, "Analog and Digital Communication: On Negation, Signification, and Meaning," in his *System and Structure: Essays on Communication and Exchange* (London: Tavistock, 1972).

20. Bergson, *Creative Evolution*, 90.

21. Ibid., 32.

22. Although it is commonly assumed that intuition is some vague feeling or sensibility, for Bergson it is a quite precise mode that refuses or precedes symbolization and representation: "We call intuition here the sympathy by which one is transported into the interior of an object in order to coincide with what there is unique and consequently inexpressible in it" (*The Creative Mind*, 190). Instead of a mere sympathy or identification, which is nothing but a psychologization or subjectivization of knowledge, Bergson wants to link intuition to an understanding of the absolute. What the intellect provides is a relative knowledge, a knowledge of things from a distance and thus from a perspective mediated by symbols, representations, and measurements, while intuition is what can provide an absolute analysis, which means one that is both internal and simple. This absolute is not understood in terms of an eternal or unchanging essence, but is rather, from the outside, a complex interplay of multiple forces and factors that, from the inside, resolves itself into a simple unity: "Seen from within, an absolute is then a simple thing; but considered from without, that is to say relative to something else, it becomes, with relation to those signs which express it, the piece of gold for which one can never make up the change" (ibid.).

Aristotle. *Politics.* Trans. H. Rackham. Cambridge: Harvard University Press, 1972.

Bacon, Francis. *The New Atlantis.* Harmondsworth: Penguin, 1974.

Bataille, Georges. *The Accursed Share.* 3 vols. Trans. Robert Hurley. New York: Zone Books, 1991.

Bataille, Georges, ed. *Encyclopædia Acephalica: Comprising the Critical Dictionary and Related Texts Edited by Georges Bataille and the Encyclopædia Da Costa.* Ed. Robert Lebel and Isabelle Waldberg. London: Atlas Press, 1995.

Bataille, Georges. *On Nietzsche.* Trans. Bruce Boone. New York: Paragon House, 1992.

Bataille, Georges. *Visions of Excess: Selected Writings 1927–1939.* Ed. and trans. Allan Stoekl. Manchester: Manchester University Press, 1985.

Batchen, Geoffrey. "Spectres of Cyberspace." *Afterimage* 23, no. 3 (November/December 1995), 4–17.

Benedikt, Michael, ed. *Cyberspace: First Steps.* Cambridge: MIT Press, 1991.

Bergson, Henri. *Creative Evolution.* Trans. Arthur Mitchell. New York: Random House, 1944.

Bergson, Henri. *The Creative Mind: An Introduction to Metaphysics.* Trans. Mabelle L. Andison. New York: Citadel Press, 1992.

Bergson, Henri. *Matter and Memory.* Trans. N. M. Paul and W. S. Palmer. New York: Zone Books, 1988.

Berkel, Ben van, and Caroline Bos. *Delinquent Visionaries.* Rotterdam: 010 Publications, 1993.

Bingham, Stephen. "The Key to Cybercity: Stephen Bingham." Interview by Brian Boigon and David Clarkson. *MSV*, no. 2 (Winter 1991–1992), 6–12.

Boigon, Brian, ed. *Culture Lab*. New York: Princeton Architectural Press, 1993.

Boundas, Constantin V. "Bergson-Deleuze: An Ontology of the Virtual." In Paul Patton, ed., *Deleuze: A Critical Reader*. Oxford: Blackwell, 1996.

Boundas, Constantin V., ed. *The Deleuze Reader*. New York: Columbia University, 1993.

Boundas, Constantin V., and Dorothea Olkowski, eds. *Gilles Deleuze and the Theatre of Philosophy*. New York: Routledge, 1994.

Braidotti, Rosi. "Toward a New Nomadism: Feminist Deleuzian Tracks; or, Metaphysics and Metabolism." In Constantin V. Boundas and Dorothea Olkowski, eds., *Gilles Deleuze and the Theatre of Philosophy*. New York: Routledge, 1994.

Butler, Rex, and Paul Patton, eds. "Dossier on Gilles Deleuze." *Agenda: Contemporary Art Magazine*, no. 33 (September 1993), 16–36.

Caillois, Roger. "Mimicry and Legendary Psychasthenia." *October*, no. 31 (1984), 17–32.

Casey, Edward. *Getting Back into Place: Toward a Renewed Understanding of the Place-World*. Bloomington: Indiana University Press, 1993.

Colombat, André Pierre. "A Thousand Trails to Work with Deleuze." *Sub-Stance* 20, no. 3 (1991), 10–23.

Colomina, Beatriz, ed. *Sexuality and Space*. New York: Princeton Architectural Press, 1992.

Davidson, Cynthia C., ed. *Anywhere*. New York: Rizzoli International Publications, 1992.

Deleuze, Gilles. "Ariadne's Mystery." *ANY*, no. 5 (1994), 8–9.

Deleuze, Gilles. *Bergsonism*. Trans. Hugh Tomlinson and Barbara Habberjam. New York: Zone Books, 1988.

Deleuze, Gilles. *Cinema 2: The Time-Image.* Trans. Hugh Tomlinson and Robert Galeta. Minneapolis: University of Minnesota Press, 1989.

Deleuze, Gilles. *Difference and Repetition.* Trans. Paul Patton. New York: Columbia University Press, 1994.

Deleuze, Gilles. "The Exhausted." *Parallax,* no. 3 (September 1996), 116–135.

Deleuze, Gilles. *The Fold: Leibniz and the Baroque.* Trans. Tom Conley. Minneapolis: University of Minnesota Press, 1993.

Deleuze, Gilles. *Foucault.* Trans. Seán Hand. Minneapolis: University of Minnesota Press, 1988.

Deleuze, Gilles. "He Stuttered." In Constantin V. Boundas and Dorothea Olkowski, eds., *Gilles Deleuze and the Theatre of Philosophy.* New York: Routledge, 1994.

Deleuze, Gilles. *Nietzsche and Philosophy.* Trans. Hugh Tomlinson. New York: Columbia University Press, 1983.

Deleuze, Gilles. *A Thousand Plateaus: Capitalism and Schizophrenia.* Trans. Brian Massumi. Minneapolis: University of Minnesota Press, 1987.

Deleuze, Gilles, and Félix Guattari. *Anti-Oedipus: Capitalism and Schizophrenia.* Trans. Robert Hurley, Mark Seem, and Helen R. Lane. Minneapolis: University of Minnesota Press, 1983.

Deleuze, Gilles, and Claire Parnet. *Dialogues.* Trans. Hugh Tomlinson and Barbara Habberjam. New York: Columbia University Press, 1987.

Derrida, Jacques. "Différance." In *Margins of Philosophy,* trans. Alan Bass. Chicago: University of Chicago Press, 1982.

Derrida, Jacques. "Faxitexture." In Cynthia C. Davidson, ed., *Anywhere.* New York: Rizzoli International Publications, 1992.

Eisenman, Peter. "Folding in Time: The Singularity of Rebstock." *Columbia Documents of Architecture and Theory: D* 2 (1993), 99–112.

Foucault, Michel. *Discipline and Punish: The Birth of the Prison*. Trans. Alan Sheridan. London: Allen Lane, 1974.

Foucault, Michel. "The Discourse on Language." In *The Archaeology of Knowledge*. New York: Harper Colophon, 1972.

Foucault, Michel. *The History of Sexuality*. Vol. 1, *An Introduction*. Trans. Robert Hurley. London: Allen Lane, 1978.

Foucault, Michel. *The Order of Things*. Trans. Alan Sheridan. London: Tavistock, 1970.

Freud, Sigmund. "The Ego and the Id." In *The Standard Edition of the Complete Psychological Works of Sigmund Freud*, ed. James Strachey. Vol. 19. Oxford: Hogarth Press, 1953.

Gilbert, Nigel, and Rosaria Conte, eds. *Artificial Societies: The Computer Simulation of Social Life*. London: University College London Press, 1995.

Girard, René. *The Scapegoat*. Trans. Yvonne Freccero. Baltimore: Johns Hopkins University Press, 1986.

Grisham, Therese. "Linguistics as an Indiscipline: Deleuze and Guattari's Pragmatics." *Sub-Stance* 20, no. 3 (1991), 36–54.

Grosz, Elizabeth. "Cyberspace, Virtuality and the Real: Some Architectural Reflections." In Cynthia C. Davidson, ed., *Anybody*. Cambridge: MIT Press, 1997.

Grosz, Elizabeth. *Space, Time and Perversion: Essays on the Politics of Bodies*. New York: Routledge, 1995.

Grosz, Elizabeth. "A Thousand Tiny Sexes: Feminism and Rhizomatics." In Constantin V. Boundas and Dorothea Olkowski, eds., *Gilles Deleuze and the Theatre of Philosophy*. New York: Routledge, 1994.

Grosz, Elizabeth. *Volatile Bodies: Toward a Corporeal Feminism*. Bloomington: Indiana University Press, 1994.

Guattari, Félix. "Space and Corporeity." *Columbia Documents of Architecture and Theory: D* 2 (1993), 139–148.

Hardt, Michael. *An Apprenticeship in Philosophy: Gilles Deleuze*. Minneapolis: University of Minnesota Press, 1993.

Heim, Michael. "Re Metaphysics of Virtual Reality." In Sandra K. Helsel and Judith P. Roth, eds., *Virtual Reality: Theory, Practice and Promise*. London: Meckler, 1991.

Helsel, Sandra K., and Judith P. Roth, eds. *Virtual Reality: Theory, Practice and Promise*. London: Meckler, 1991.

Hollier, Denis. "Mimesis and Castration 1937." *October*, no. 31 (1984), 3–16.

Ingraham, Catherine. "Moving Targets." *Columbia Documents of Architecture and Theory: D* 2 (1993), 112–122.

Irigaray, Luce. *An Ethics of Sexual Difference*. Trans. Carolyn Burke and Gillian C. Gill. Ithaca: Cornell University Press, 1993.

Irigaray, Luce. "Où et comment habiter?" *Les Cahiers du Grif*, issue on *Jouir*, no. 26 (March 1983).

Irigaray, Luce. *Speculum of the Other Woman*. Trans. Gillian C. Gill. Ithaca: Cornell University Press, 1985.

Irigaray, Luce. *This Sex Which Is Not One*. Trans. Catherine Porter with Carolyn Burke. Ithaca: Cornell University Press, 1985.

Irigaray, Luce. "Volume without Contours." In *The Irigaray Reader*, ed. Margaret Whitford. Oxford: Blackwell, 1991.

James, William. *A Pluralistic Universe: Hibbert Lectures at Manchester College on the Present Situation of Philosophy*. Lincoln: University of Nebraska Press, 1996.

James, William. *Pragmatism and Four Essays from The Meaning of Truth*. Cleveland: Meridian Books, 1970.

Lacan, Jacques. *Écrits: A Selection*. Trans. Alan Sheridan. London: Tavistock, 1977.

Lacan, Jacques. "Some Reflections on the Ego." *International Journal of Psychoanalysis*, no. 34 (1953).

Le Doeuff, Michèle. "Daydream in Utopia." In Le Doeuff, *The Philosophical Imaginary*, trans. Colin Gordon. Stanford: Stanford University Press, 1989.

Le Doeuff, Michèle. "The Polysemy of Atopian Discourse." In Le Doeuff, *The Philosophical Imaginary*, trans. Colin Gordon. Stanford: Stanford University Press, 1989.

Lingis, Alphonso. *The Community of Those Who Have Nothing in Common*. Bloomington: Indiana University Press, 1994.

Massumi, Brian. "Everywhere You Want to Be: Introduction to Fear." In Brian Massumi, ed., *The Politics of Everyday Fear*. Minneapolis: University of Minnesota Press, 1993.

Massumi, Brian. *A User's Guide to Capitalism and Schizophrenia: Deviations from Deleuze and Guattari*. Cambridge: MIT Press, 1992.

Mitchell, William J. *City of Bits: Space, Place, and the Infobahn*. Cambridge: MIT Press, 1995.

More, Thomas. *Utopia*. Cambridge: Cambridge University Press, 1975.

Morris, Meaghan. "Great Moments in Social Climbing: King Kong and the Human Fly." In Beatriz Colomina, ed., *Sexuality and Space*. New York: Princeton Architectural Press, 1992.

Nixon, Mark. "De Recombinant Architectura." *21.C* (January 1996), 46–64.

Novak, Marcos. "Liquid Architectures in Cyberspace." In Michael Benedikt, ed., *Cyberspace: First Steps*. Cambridge: MIT Press, 1991.

Pitkin, Hanna Fenichel. *The Attack of the Blob: Hannah Arendt's Concept of the Social*. Chicago: University of Chicago Press, 1998.

Plato. *The Laws*. Trans. A. E. Taylor. In *The Collected Dialogues of Plato*. New York: Pantheon Books, 1966.

Plato. *The Republic*. Trans. G. M. Gude. Indianapolis: Hackett Publishing, 1974.

Plato. *Timaeus and Critias*. Trans. Desmond Lee. Harmondsworth: Penguin, 1983.

Rajchman, John. "Anywhere and Nowhere." In Cynthia C. Davidson, ed., *Anywhere*. New York: Rizzoli International Publications, 1992.

Rajchman, John. *Constructions.* Cambridge: MIT Press, 1998.

Rajchman, John. "The Earth Is Called Light." *ANY,* no. 5 (1994), 12–13.

Rajchman, John. "Lightness: A Concept in Architecture." *ANY,* no. 5 (1994), 5–6.

Rheingold, Howard. *Virtual Reality.* New York: Summit Books, 1991.

Rorty, Richard. *Consequences of Pragmatism.* Brighton, Eng.: Harvester Press, 1982.

Ross, Andrew. *Strange Weather: Culture, Science and Technology in the Age of Limits.* London: Verso, 1991.

Schilder, Paul. *The Image and Appearance of the Human Body.* New York: International Universities Press, 1978.

Simondon, Gilbert. "The Genesis of the Individual." Trans. Mark Cohen and Sanford Kwinter. In Jonathan Crary and Sanford Kwinter, eds., *Incorporations.* New York: Zone Books, 1992.

Stone, Allucquère Roseanne. "Virtual Systems." In Jonathan Crary and Sanford Kwinter, eds., *Incorporations.* New York: Zone Books, 1992.

Thomsen, Christian W. *Visionary Architecture: From Babylon to Virtual Reality.* Munich: Prestel-Verlag, 1994.

Virilio, Paul. "The Law of Proximity." *Columbia Documents of Architecture and Theory: D* 2 (1993), 123–138.

Watson, Sophie, and Katherine Gibson, eds. *Postmodern Cities and Spaces.* Oxford: Blackwell, 1995.

Whitford, Margaret. *Luce Irigaray: Philosophy in the Feminine.* London: Routledge, 1991.

Wilden, Anthony. *System and Structure: Essays on Communication and Exchange.* London: Tavistock, 1972.

Index

Persons

Topics